A GIFT FOR:

Ms. Sullivan

FROM:

Rilynn

WIT AND WISDOM FROM THE ROAD

by Lou Harry

Hallmark

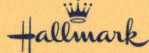

Wit and Wisdom from the Road

Copyright © 2017 by Appleseed Press Book Publishers LLC.

This is an officially licensed book by Cider Mill Press Book Publishers LLC.

All rights reserved under the Pan-American and International Copyright Conventions.

This edition published in 2017 by Hallmark Gift Books, a division of Hallmark Cards, Inc., Kansas City, MO 64141 under license from Cider Mill Press.

Visit us on the Web at Hallmark.com.

No part of this book may be reproduced in whole or in part, scanned, photocopied, recorded, distributed in any printed or electronic form, or reproduced in any manner whatsoever, or by any information storage and retrieval system now known or hereafter invented, without express written permission of the publisher, except in the case of brief quotations embodied in critical articles and reviews.

The scanning, uploading, and distribution of this book via the Internet or via any other means without permission of the publisher is illegal and punishable by law. Please support authors' rights, and do not participate in or encourage piracy of copyrighted materials.

Design by: Alicia Freile, Tango Media
Typography: Clarendon, Journal, and Whitney
All images are used under official license from Shutterstock.com

ISBN: 978-1-63059-860-0
BOK1319

Made in China
0518

NEW ENGLAND

Maine

Pit Stop:
Acadia National Park

You've got forty-seven thousand acres to choose from in Maine's only national park, commissioned by John D. Rockefeller in 1915. To say that it's topographically varied is an understatement. Take in its rocky coastline, its forests, its fields, and its mountains while keeping an eye out for peregrine falcons and herons above, moose and salamanders on land, and whales and seals off the coast.

ADDED STOPS IN MAINE

1. Fort Knox, Prospect
2. Desert of Maine, Freeport
3. Boothbay Harbor
4. Kennebunkport
5. Portland Head Light, Cape Elizabeth

FUN FACT: At their peak, 95 percent of all American-made toothpicks—over 75 billion annually—were manufactured in Strong, Maine.

Lighthouse at Acadia National Park

Massachusetts

Pit Stop:
The Freedom Trail, Boston

One of the country's most iconic pathways, this trail connects sixteen of the most important historical sites in the United States. From Boston Common and the Massachusetts State House to the Paul Revere House and Old North Church, this trail is both a sightseeing adventure and a history lesson. Pick your favorite landmarks and drive to them, or park your car and walk the whole two-and-a-half-mile trail for a nice leg stretch.

Paul Revere Statue and Old North Church in Boston

Added Stops in Massachusetts

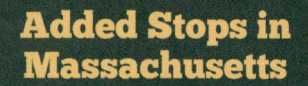

1.
Fenway Park, Boston

2.
Plymouth Rock, Plymouth

3.
The Mount (Edith Wharton's Home), Lenox

4.
Norman Rockwell Museum, Stockbridge

5.
Faneuil Hall Marketplace, Boston

FUN FACT: No surprise here—the Massachusetts state dog is the Boston Terrier.

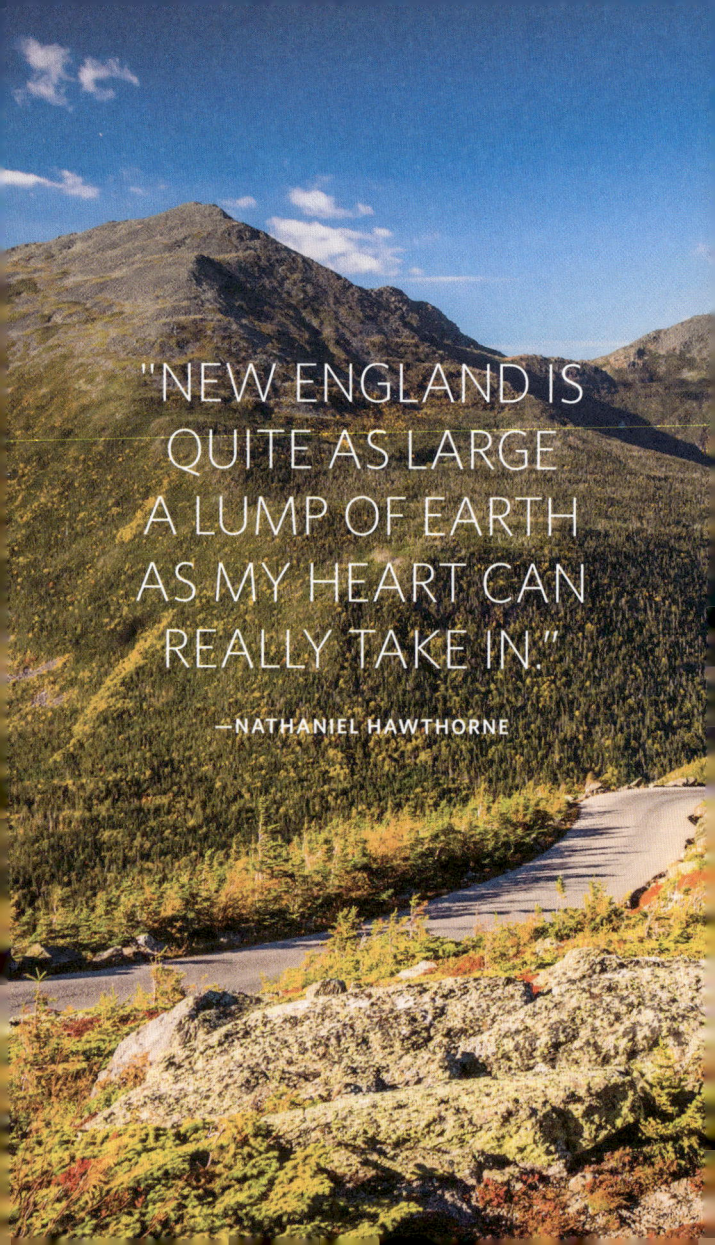

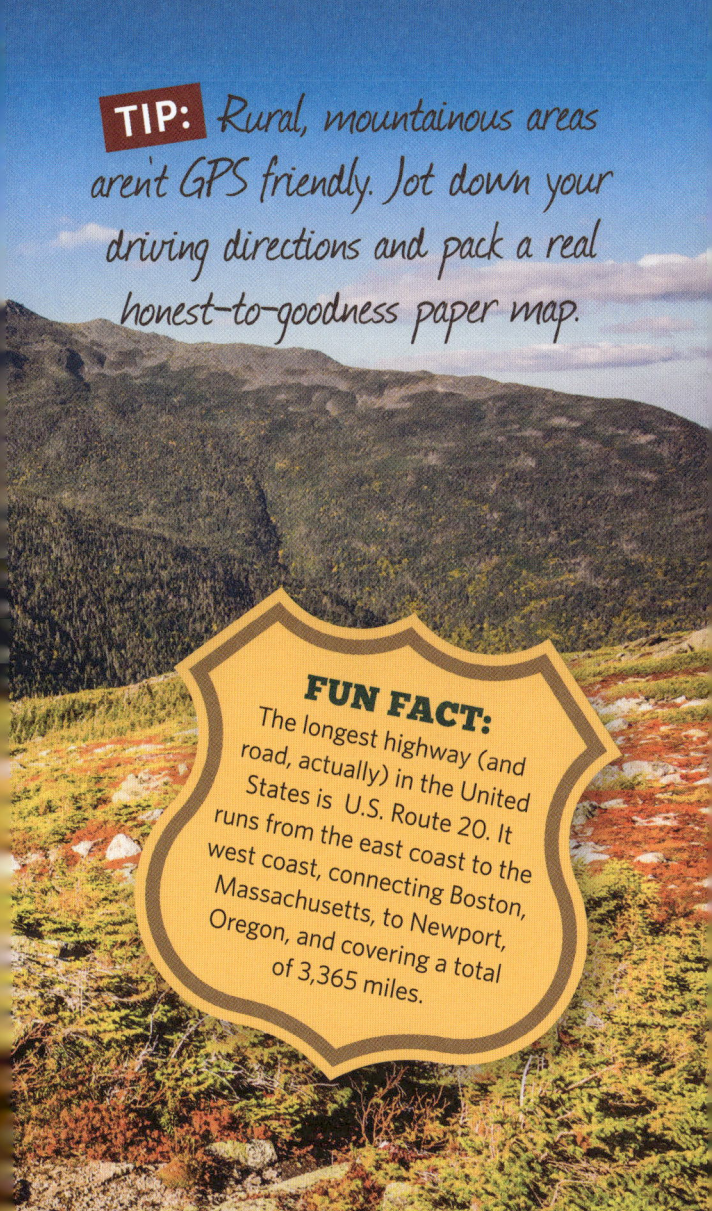

TIP: Rural, mountainous areas aren't GPS friendly. Jot down your driving directions and pack a real honest-to-goodness paper map.

FUN FACT:
The longest highway (and road, actually) in the United States is U.S. Route 20. It runs from the east coast to the west coast, connecting Boston, Massachusetts, to Newport, Oregon, and covering a total of 3,365 miles.

New Hampshire

Pit Stop:
Portsmouth

Whether you're driving through Market Square or taking in the views of the Piscataqua River from Memorial Bridge, this historic seaport town is the perfect road trip destination. From the Portsmouth Navy Yard to the still-active tugboats, the town prospers from the harbor. Stroll or drive along the water for a unique view of this thriving port.

ADDED STOPS IN NEW HAMPSHIRE

1. Santa's Village, Jefferson
2. The Currier Museum of Art, Manchester
3. USS *Albacore* Museum, Portsmouth
4. Wright Museum of World War II, Wolfeboro
5. Mount Washington Cog Railway, Bretton Woods

FUN FACT: Earl Tupper invented Tupperware in Berlin, New Hampshire.

Tugboats in Portsmouth

Vermont

Pit Stop:
Ben & Jerry's Factory, Waterbury

It's difficult to make a spontaneous stop at a ski resort, especially if you haven't packed all the requisite equipment. On the other hand, it's difficult *not* to make a spontaneous stop at the Ben & Jerry's Factory, where a thirty-minute tour leads to a full-service scoop shop. You can add on a woodland snowshoe tour that includes the "Flavor Graveyard," which pays tribute to retired flavors.

ADDED STOPS IN VERMONT

1. Green Mountain National Forest, Rutland
2. Lake Champlain Maritime Museum, Vergennes
3. Hildene, the Lincoln Family Home, Manchester
4. Vermont Marble Museum, Proctor
5. Ethan Allen Homestead Museum, Burlington

FUN FACT: According to *The Economist*, about three-quarters of the cars that Rolls-Royce has ever produced are still on the road today. Talk about a good investment.

The Ben & Jerry's Factory

"The gladdest moment in human life, me thinks, is a departure into unknown lands."

—SIR RICHARD BURTON

Rhode Island

Pit Stop:
Newport Mansions, Newport

Immaculately preserved, the mansions of Newport are like a time machine into the fabulous lives of the Astors, the Vanderbilts, and other millionaires of the day. For jaw-dropping Gilded Age opulence, visit The Breakers, the grandest of all of Newport, Rhode Island's summer "cottages."

The Breakers in Newport

ADDED STOPS IN RHODE ISLAND

1. The Big Blue Bug, Providence
2. The Green Animals Topiary, Portsmouth
3. Musée Patamécanique, Bristol
4. Newport Cliff Walk, Newport
5. The International Tennis Hall of Fame, Newport

Connecticut

Pit Stop:
Mark Twain House & Museum, Hartford

Stop at the Mark Twain House & Museum to celebrate the life and writings of the man born with the name Samuel Clemens. This quintessentially American writer is best known for the classic novels *The Adventures of Tom Sawyer* and *The Adventures of Huckleberry Finn*.

ADDED STOPS IN CONNECTICUT

1. Gillette Castle, East Haddam
2. The Frog Bridge, Willimantic
3. Cove Island State Park, Stamford
4. Mystic Seaport
5. Wadsworth Atheneum Museum of Art, Hartford

The Mark Twain House and Museum

"I have found out that there ain't no surer way to find out whether you like people or hate them than to travel with them."

—MARK TWAIN, *TOM SAWYER ABROAD*

MID-ATLANTIC

New York

**Pit Stop:
Ellis Island Immigration Museum,
New York City**

The beauty of an all-American road trip is in its diversity—urban and rural, mountains and prairies, serious and silly, from sea to shining sea—just as is the case with the American people. A road trip can start from anywhere. But for many of us, our American story goes back to Ellis Island. Nearly half of all Americans are descended from the twelve million immigrants who passed through Ellis Island between 1891 and 1954. If you start—or stop—in the Big Apple, take a ferry to get to the Statue of Liberty Monument and the Ellis Island Immigration Museum.

Ellis Island Immigration Museum

Added Stops in New York

1.
Niagara Falls State Park, Niagara Falls

2.
Corning Museum of Glass, Corning

3.
Olympic Torch, Lake Placid

4.
Brooklyn Bridge, New York City

5.
Empire State Building, New York City

"ITS LIFE IS SO INTENSE AND SO VARIED, AND SO FULL OF MANIFOLD POSSIBILITIES, THAT IT HAS A SPECIAL AND PECULIAR FASCINATION."

—THEODORE ROOSEVELT, *NEW YORK*

Pennsylvania

Pit Stop:
Independence Hall, Philadelphia

It's impossible not to feel the pull of history when you step into the very room where the Declaration of Independence was signed. Bonus: From this anchoring stop at Independence National Historical Park, you are just steps away from attractions as old as the Liberty Bell and as new as the National Constitution Center.

Independence Hall National Historical Park

ADDED STOPS IN PENNSYLVANIA

1. Gettysburg National Military Park
2. The Andy Warhol Museum, Pittsburgh
3. Flight 93 National Memorial, Stoystown
4. Philadelphia Museum of Art, Philadelphia
5. Longwood Gardens, Kennett Square

FUN FACT:
The Philadelphia Eagles and the Pittsburgh Steelers merged for one season, in 1943, because so many players were otherwise engaged in WWII.

TIP: Be respectful when traveling through Pennsylvania Dutch country. Remember, these are real people with real lives, not actors there for the benefit of tourists. Ask permission before taking pictures and be ready to take "no" for an answer.

TIP: The longer the trip, the looser the scheduling should be. That doesn't mean avoiding specifics; it means not letting an out-of-your-control change ruin your trip. Raining when you were planning a day at the beach? Plan B . . . or C . . . might be just the activity you need.

New Jersey

Pit Stop:
Wildwood

This South Jersey resort island not only has some of the largest beaches in the country—brace yourself for a long trek from your first footsteps in the sand to the shoreline—but it also features a thrill-packed boardwalk. Bonus: It has embraced and celebrated its unique, doo-wop style architecture. Stop in at the Doo Wop Experience and Neon Sign Garden for a little history and a lot of nostalgic fun.

Morey's Piers in Wildwood

ADDED STOPS IN NEW JERSEY

1. Institute Woods, Princeton
2. Thomas Edison National Historical Park, West Orange
3. Victorian Cape May
4. Troy Meadows, Parsippany-Troy Hills
5. Liberty Science Center, Jersey City

Albert Einstein used to stroll through Institute Woods.

"Camden was originally an accident—but I shall never be sorry I was left over in Camden! It has brought me blessed returns."

—WALT WHITMAN

MARVIN GARDENS

$280

GO TO JAIL

FUN FACT:
Monopoly's properties are named after Atlantic City and surrounding locations. There is one spelling error, though. Marvin Gardens should actually be Marven Gardens, a neighborhood just down the island in Margate City.

Delaware

Pit Stop:
Winterthur Museum, Gardens and Library, Winterthur

As you might expect since this is Delaware, the Winterthur Museum was founded by a du Pont—Henry Francis du Pont, to be exact. Pronounced "winter-tour," it's now the go-to museum in the country for American decorative arts. And the acres of outdoor gardens are as interesting as what you find inside (which includes lectures, workshops, performances, and a research library).

Gardens at the Winterthur Estate

ADDED STOPS IN DELAWARE

1. Rehoboth Beach and Boardwalk
2. DuPont Mansions, Wilmington
3. Fort Delaware, Delaware City
4. Dover International Speedway and Monster Mile, Dover
5. Bombay Hook National Wildlife Refuge, Smyrna

FUN FACT: Delaware is nicknamed "The First State" because it was the first to ratify the U.S. Constitution.

TIP: The price on your purchases is the price you pay when shopping in Delaware. The state has no sales tax.

Maryland

Pit Stop:
National Aquarium, Baltimore

About twenty thousand creatures are swimming around at this Baltimore Inner Harbor hotspot. More than just a collection of populated tanks, the National Aquarium includes areas simulating an Atlantic coral reef, the Australian outback, a tropical rainforest, and more. When was the last time you petted a stingray?

The National Aquarium

ADDED STOPS IN MARYLAND

1. American Visionary Art Museum, Baltimore
2. Fort McHenry National Monument and Historic Shrine, Baltimore
3. Antietam National Battlefield, Sharpsburg
4. Chesapeake and Ohio Canal National Historic Park, Hagerstown
5. Assateague Island National Seashore, Berlin

FUN FACT:
Baltimore's annual Kinetic Sculpture Race is an eight-hour challenge in which human-powered works of art have to cover fourteen miles—including parts of the Chesapeake Bay and through sand and mud.

TIP: Don't try to pet or feed the wild horses of Assateague Island. They bite.

Washington, D.C.

Pit Stop:
The Smithsonian Museums

The Smithsonian isn't just one museum—it's nineteen of them, plus research facilities and the National Zoo. You can spend the bulk of a vacation in any one of them. Most are along the National Mall, including one of the two National Air and Space Museums, the Natural History museum, and the American History museum. For an esoteric twist, pay a visit to the Hirshhorn Museum and Sculpture Garden. Best of all: Smithsonian museums are free to the public.

The National Museum of Natural History

"I NEVER FORGET THAT I LIVE IN A HOUSE OWNED BY ALL THE AMERICAN PEOPLE AND THAT I HAVE BEEN GIVEN THEIR TRUST."

—FRANKLIN D. ROOSEVELT

TIP: Just because you've arrived by car doesn't mean your car is your best choice for every excursion while in a city. Cost—and headaches—often can be drastically reduced by using a cab, driver service, or bus. And don't be shy about asking at your hotel about shuttle service to area attractions.

ADDED STOPS IN WASHINGTON, D.C.

1. National Building Museum
2. Lincoln Memorial
3. Vietnam Veterans Memorial
4. National Archives
5. United States Holocaust Memorial Museum

FUN FACT:
The original phone number for the White House in 1878 was the number 1.

"I seldom go to the place I set out for."

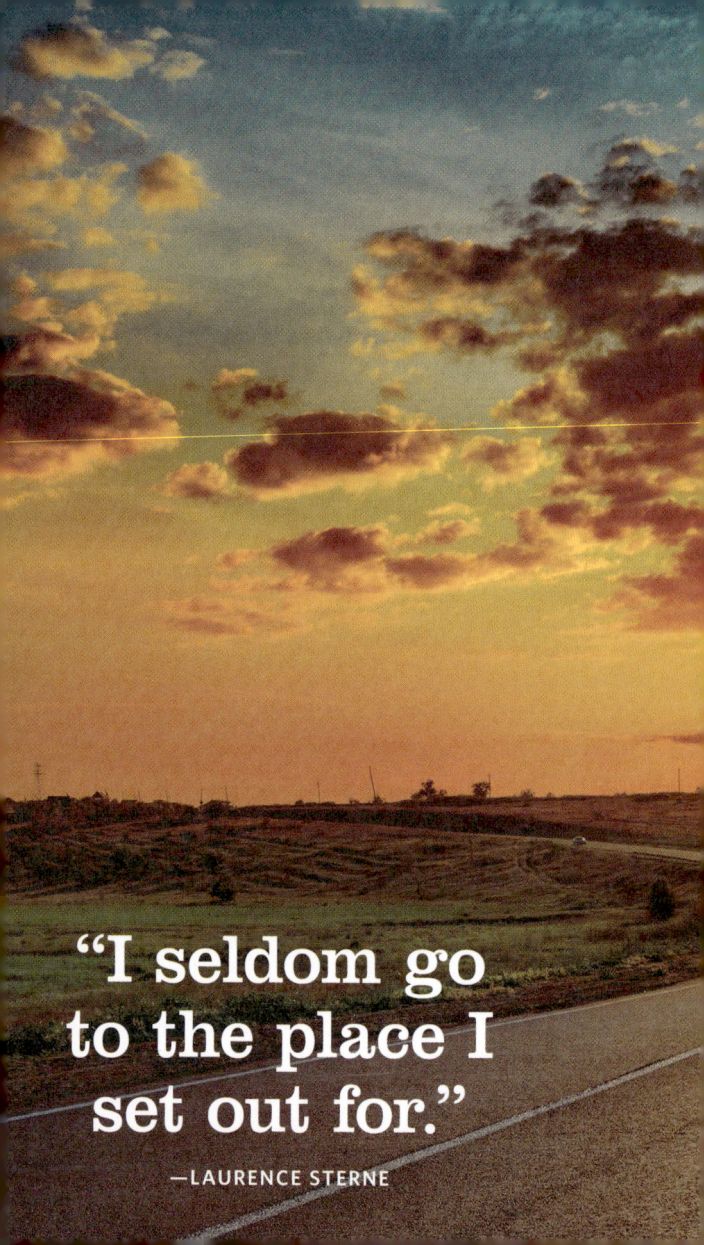

—LAURENCE STERNE

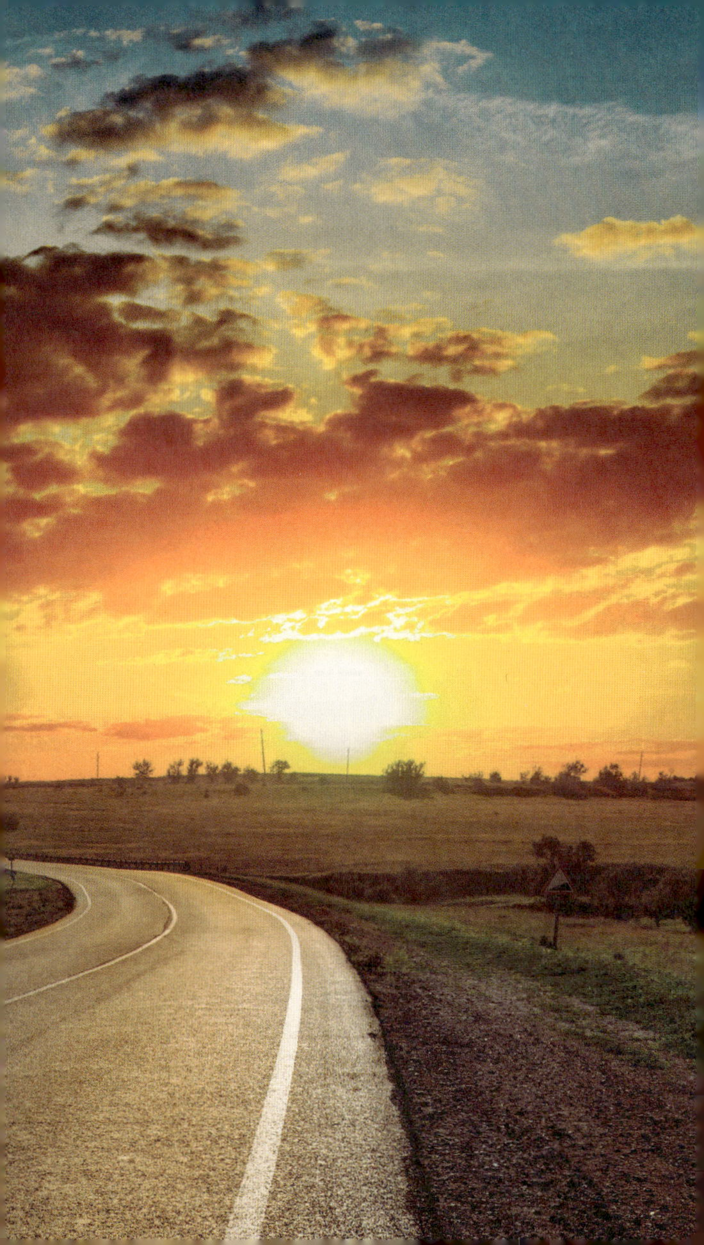

Virginia

Pit Stop:
Colonial Williamsburg

The former capital of Virginia is populated with costumed interpreters to help you forget that cell phone in your pocket and lose yourself in history. Colonial gardens and folk and decorative arts museums add to the experience. And if you need to pick up the pace a bit, there's a Busch Gardens theme park nearby.

ADDED STOPS IN VIRGINIA

1. Mount Vernon
2. Arlington National Cemetery, Arlington
3. Monticello, Charlottesville
4. The Pentagon, Arlington
5. Shenandoah National Park

FUN FACT: Eight U.S. Presidents—including five of the first ten—were born in Virginia, earning it the nickname "Mother of Presidents."

Colonial Williamsburg

TIP: By all means, be navigationally adventurous. Just remember that not every back road is an interesting one. As much as we might romanticize off-highway travel, sometimes taking what looks like a scenic route is just a series of traffic lights and chain restaurants. Do a little homework before straying from the shortest distance to your destination.

"The *Natural bridge*, the most sublime of Nature's works ... so beautiful an arch, so elevated, so light, and springing as it were up to heaven, the rapture of the spectator is really indescribable!"

—THOMAS JEFFERSON ON ROCKBRIDGE COUNTY, VIRGINIA

West Virginia

Pit Stop:
Prabhupada's Palace of Gold, Moundsville

What will future generations think of this jaw-dropping structure, built as a residence for the founder of the Society for Krishna Consciousness, A.C. Bhaktivedanta Swami Prabhupada? Alas, he died before move-in day. The palace, rose gardens, and more than one hundred fountains are now open to the public.

ADDED STOPS IN WEST VIRGINIA

1. Harpers Ferry National Historical Park
2. Aerial tram at Hawk's Nest State Park, Ansted
3. West Virginia Penitentiary, a retired prison offering tours, Moundsville
4. Greenbrier Resort (and Congressional bunker), White Sulphur Springs
5. World's Largest Teapot, Chester

FUN FACT:
The world's fully steerable radio telescope is in Greenbank, West Virginia. It also is credited as the world's largest movable land object.

Harpers Ferry National Historic Park

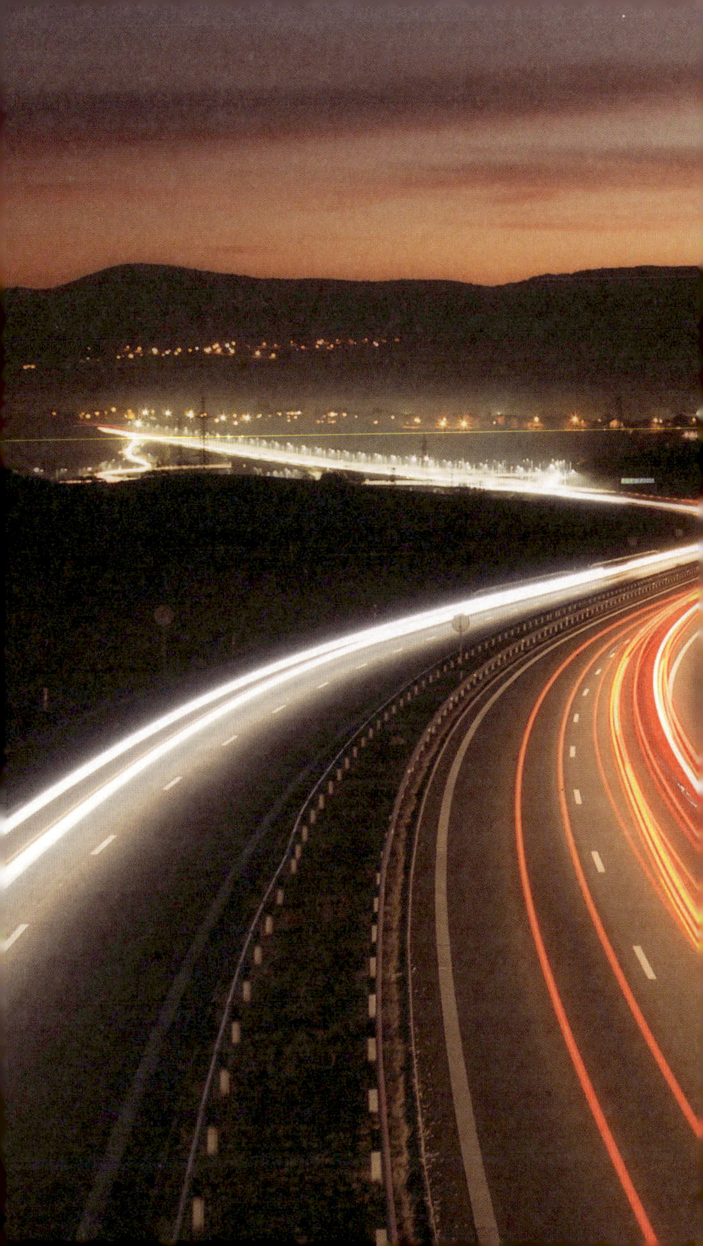

"There are no foreign lands. It is the traveler only who is foreign."

–ROBERT LOUIS STEVENSON

North Carolina

Pit Stop:
Biltmore Estate, Asheville

George Vanderbilt's modest—okay, not so modest—two hundred fifty-room home is open to the public for touring, as are the gardens and grounds designed by landscape architect Frederick Law Olmstead. Highlights include paintings by Renoir and Sargent, a ten-thousand-volume library, and a banquet hall with seventy-foot ceilings.

The Biltmore Estate

ADDED STOPS IN NORTH CAROLINA

1. Wright Brothers National Memorial, Kitty Hawk
2. Outer Banks
3. Great Smoky Mountains National Park
4. Roanoke Island
5. NASCAR Hall of Fame, Charlotte

FUN FACT:

Depending on the weather, the sand dunes at Jockey's Ridge can stand between eighty and one hundred feet high, making it the largest dune system in the eastern United States.

South Carolina

Pit Stop:
USS *Yorktown*, Charleston

The USS *Yorktown* aircraft carrier, docked at Patriots Point in Charleston Harbor, not only saw active duty in both World War II and the Vietnam War, it also was the vessel that recovered the Apollo 8 astronauts. The tourable ship is the centerpiece of a naval and maritime tourism area that includes aircraft ranging from anti-submarine helicopters to the F-14A Tomcat. And don't miss the Medal of Honor Museum.

The USS Yorktown docked in Charleston

ADDED STOPS IN SOUTH CAROLINA

1. Myrtle Beach SkyWheel, Myrtle Beach
2. Charleston Historic District
3. Hilton Head Island
4. Fort Sumter, Charleston
5. The Institute for Greatly Endangered and Rare Species, North Myrtle Beach

TIP: In the Carolinas, college sports are approached with greater intensity than professional sports. Time your road trip to take in a football game.

FUN FACT: South Carolina produces more peaches than any other state in the East—including Georgia.

Georgia

**Pit Stop:
Martin Luther King, Jr. National Historic Site and The King Center, Atlanta**

While stops include the home where Dr. Martin Luther King was born and the church where he became a co-pastor, these popular Atlanta destinations are as much about the present and the future as they are about the past. For a preview, you can browse from among nearly one million documents in The King Center's collection online.

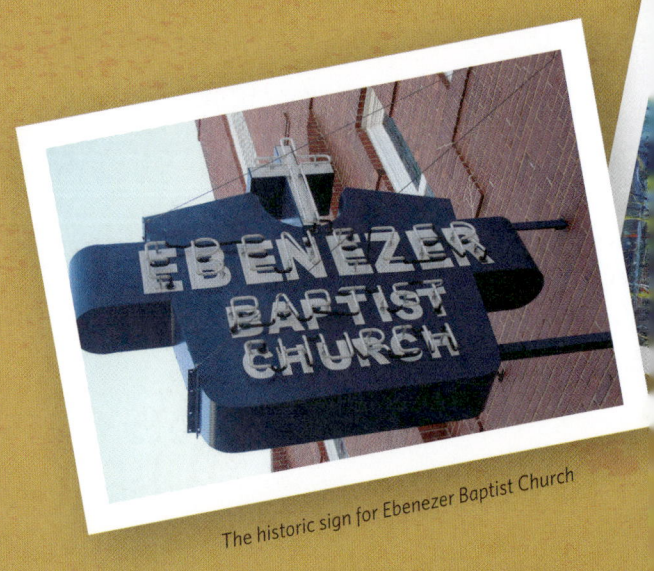

The historic sign for Ebenezer Baptist Church

TIP: Be specific when you try using your navigator in Atlanta. There are dozens of streets that include the word "Peachtree."

Martin Luther King, Jr. mural at the National Historic Site

Added Stops in Georgia

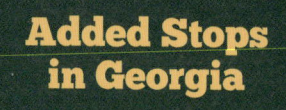

1. World of Coca-Cola, Atlanta

2. Centennial Olympic Park, Atlanta

3. Rock City, Lookout Mountain

4. College Football Hall of Fame, Atlanta

5. Bonaventure Cemetery, Savannah

Bonaventure Cemetery was the setting that John Berendt's nonfiction book *Midnight in the Garden of Good and Evil* made famous.

FUN FACT: The Atlanta dining landmark The Varsity sells four miles of hot dogs a day.

Tennessee

Pit Stop:
Nashville

Nashville is home to a plethora of stops for music lovers—and you don't have to be a hardcore country fan to appreciate it. Not only is there Opryland USA and the Ryman Auditorium (the two homes for the Grand Ole Opry live radio telecast), but also the Country Music Hall of Fame and Museum, the Musicians Hall of Fame, and tunes coming out of just about every building along downtown's Music Row and beyond.

The Grand Ole Opry

ADDED STOPS IN TENNESSEE

1. Beale Street Historic District, Memphis
2. Andrew Jackson's Hermitage, Nashville
3. National Civil Rights Museum, Memphis
4. Dollywood, Pigeon Forge
5. Graceland, Memphis

FUN FACT: On the air since 1925, the Grand Ole Opry is the world's longest continuously running live radio program. Book your tickets in advance.

Elvis Presley's grave in Graceland

"The only way to be sure of catching a train is to miss the one before it."

—G.K. CHESTERTON

Kentucky

Pit Stop:
Churchill Downs, Louisville

Of course, the ideal is to get to Churchill Downs for the Kentucky Derby. But just because that's an option only once a year doesn't give you an excuse to bypass one of the best-known sporting arenas in the country. Not only can you wager on the ponies, but you can also visit the Kentucky Derby Museum, and take a "barn and backside" tour before arriving at your day's finish line.

Entrance to Churchill Downs

FUN FACT:
Kentucky, originally part of Virginia, didn't become its own state until 1792.

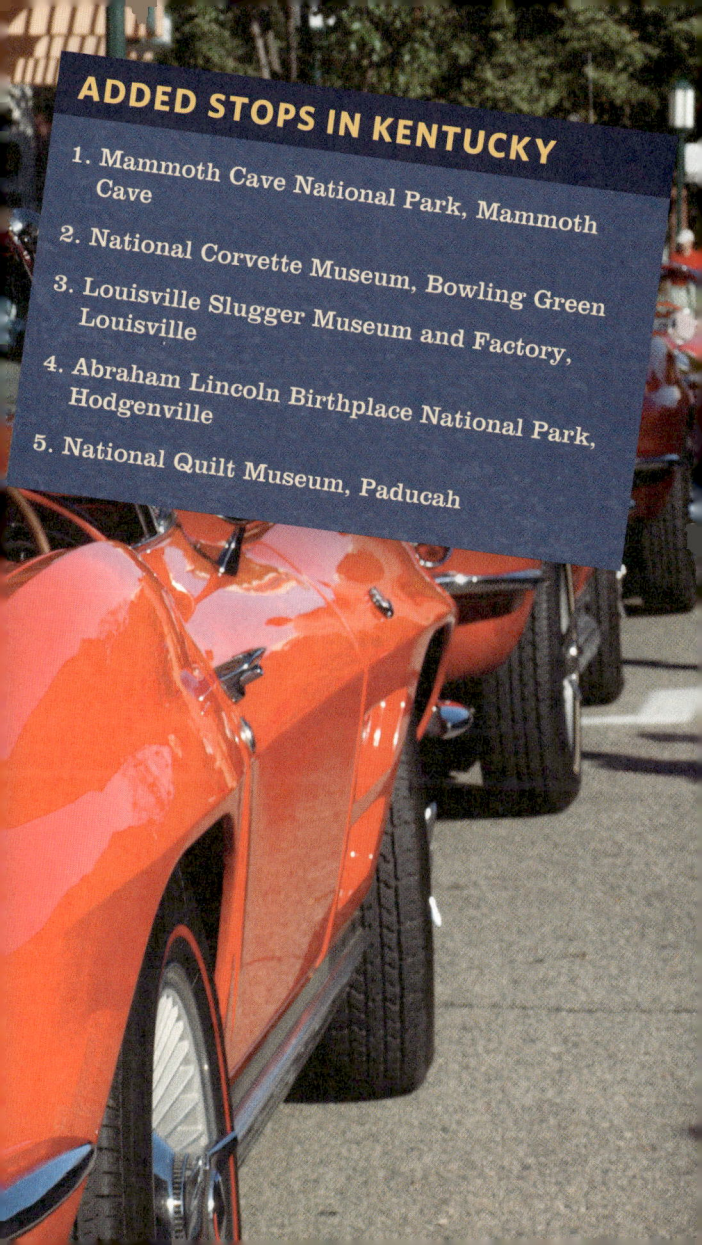

ADDED STOPS IN KENTUCKY

1. Mammoth Cave National Park, Mammoth Cave
2. National Corvette Museum, Bowling Green
3. Louisville Slugger Museum and Factory, Louisville
4. Abraham Lincoln Birthplace National Park, Hodgenville
5. National Quilt Museum, Paducah

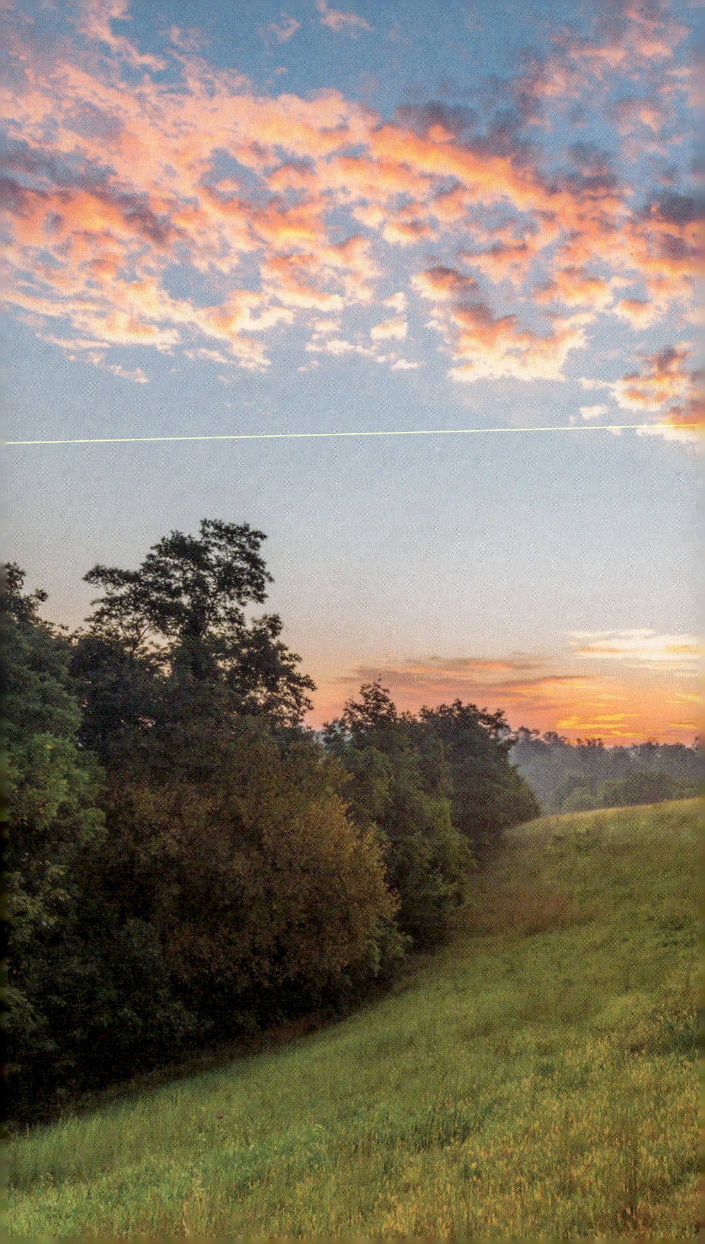

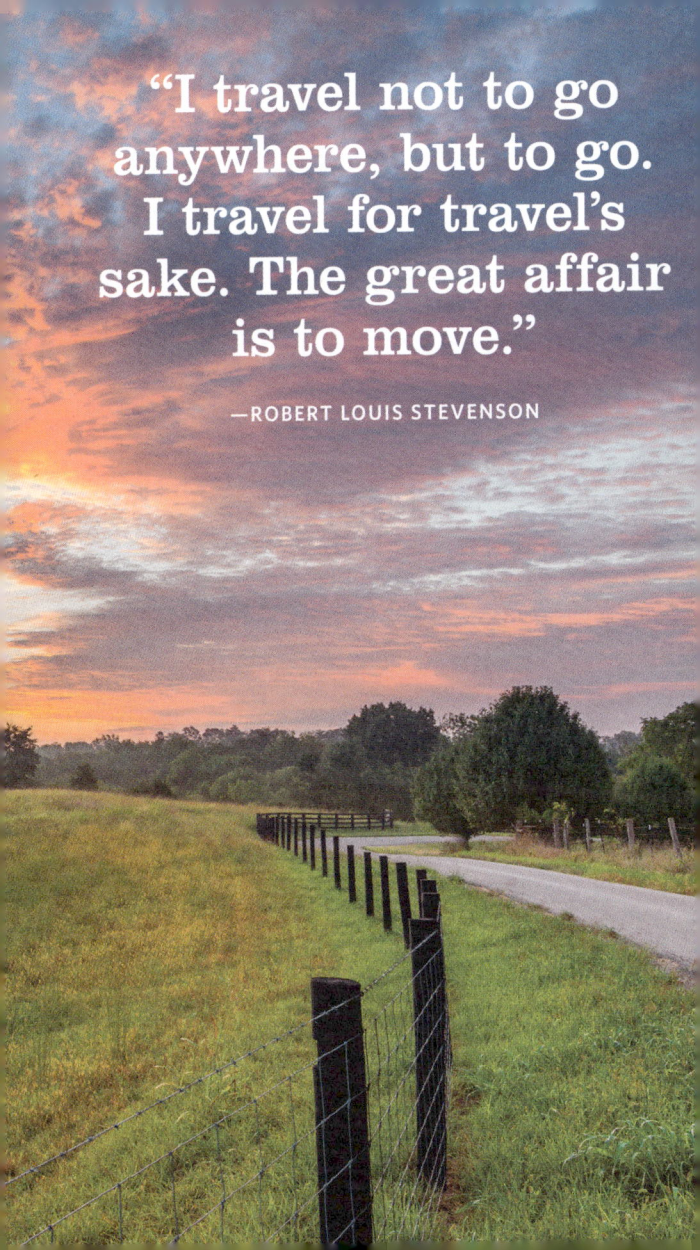

"I travel not to go anywhere, but to go. I travel for travel's sake. The great affair is to move."

—ROBERT LOUIS STEVENSON

GULF STATES

Florida

Pit Stop:
Disney World, Orlando

According to *Travel + Leisure* magazine, Walt Disney World's Magic Kingdom is the most-visited ticketed attraction in the country. There are good reasons for that. Yes, the lines are long and the price is high, but there's nothing in the world like a stroll down Main Street U.S.A. and a meet-and-greet with Mickey. And that's before you get to the world-class rides here and at the rest of the Disney parks.

ADDED STOPS IN FLORIDA

1. Everglades National Park
2. Universal Studios, Orlando
3. National Naval Aviation Museum, Pensacola
4. Kennedy Space Center, Titusville
5. South Beach, Miami

FUN FACT: It is illegal in Florida to bother a manatee.

Entrance to the Magic Kingdom section of Walt Disney World

TIP: Sometimes you may need the comfort of a familiar eatery. But try to take advantage of local eateries. You can find great locally owned choices in just about every city, and across all price points.

"The soul of a journey is liberty, perfect liberty, to think, feel, do just as one pleases."

—WILLIAM HAZLITT

Alabama

Pit Stop:
U.S. Space & Rocket Center, Huntsville

The hows and whys of space travel are explored at this Smithsonian affiliate, which also serves as the official visitors' center for NASA's Marshall Space Flight Center. The collection includes the original Mercury and Gemini capsule trainers, the Apollo 16 "Casper" capsule, and loads of interactives and space travel simulators.

Space shuttle in Huntsville

ADDED STOPS IN TENNESSEE

1. Talladega Superspeedway
2. Tuskegee Airmen National Historic Site
3. Vulcan Park & Museum, Birmingham
4. Edmund Pettus Bridge, Selma
5. Alabama Shakespeare Festival, Montgomery

FUN FACT:
Coal, iron ore, and limestone are all required to make iron—and the only place in the world where all can be found within a ten-mile radius is Birmingham.

TIP: Here are five things to keep in your trunk's emergency kit:

- flashlight
- blanket
- gallon jug of water
- flare
- first-aid kit

Mississippi

Pit Stop:
Vicksburg National Military Park, Vicksburg

Indoor and outdoor exhibits, plus living-history demonstrations June through August, bring visitors to a better understanding of a crucial Civil War turning point. You can opt for a self-guided driving tour or take advantage of licensed park tour guides.

Cannon at Vicksburg National Military Park

Added Stops in Mississippi

1.
Mississippi Freedom Trail

2.
Delta Blues Museum, Clarksdale

3.
William Faulkner's Rowan Oak Home, Oxford

4.
Eudora Welty House and Garden, Jackson

5.
B.B. King Museum and Delta Interpretive Center, Indianola

FUN FACT:
The Mississippi River flows through ten states. Slovenian swimmer Martin Strel took sixty-eight days to swim its entire length in 2002.

TIP: Mississippi has a rich literary tradition. While you may have already sampled the words of William Faulkner and John Grisham, consider adding Eudora Welty, Richard Wright, Walker Percy, Richard Price, and Shelby Foote to your reading list.

Louisiana

Pit Stop:
The French Quarter, New Orleans

In some cities, the locals wouldn't go near the top tourist attractions. But locals and visitors alike appreciate the magic of New Orleans's French Quarter. Here, outstanding music and world-class cuisine contribute to an every-day-is-a-party atmosphere. Of course, that spirit intensifies every year at Mardi Gras when beads become the currency of choice (and the kids should be left at home).

The corner of Orleans Street and Bourbon Street in New Orleans

ADDED STOPS IN LOUISIANA

1. Jean Lafitte National Historical Park and Preserve, New Orleans
2. Honey Island Swamp, St. Tammany Parish
3. Old Louisville State Capitol, Baton Rouge
4. Audubon Nature Institute, New Orleans
5. Oak Alley Plantation, Vacherie

FUN FACT: "Saturday Night Live" broadcast its only live-on-location episode from New Orleans during Mardi Gras.

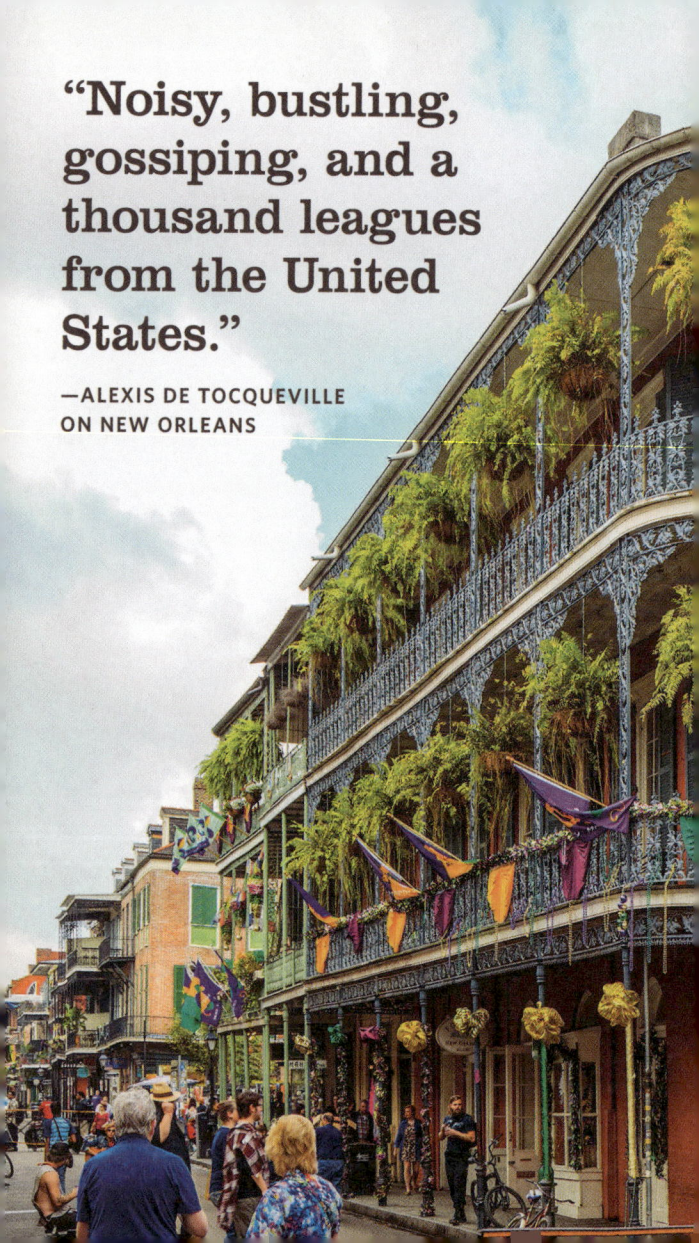

"Noisy, bustling, gossiping, and a thousand leagues from the United States."

—ALEXIS DE TOCQUEVILLE ON NEW ORLEANS

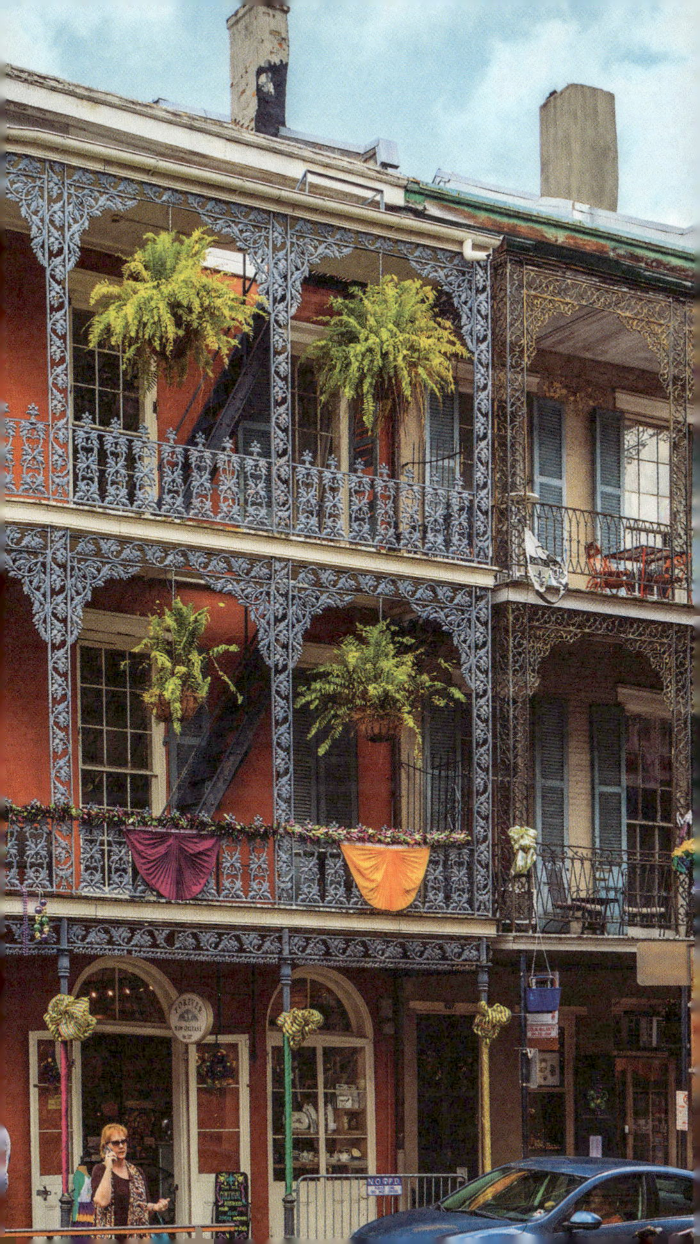

Texas

Pit Stop:
The Alamo, San Antonio

Davy Crockett fought here. Pee-wee Herman went looking for his missing bicycle here. And many a myth has been created around what started as Mission San Antonio de Valero in 1718. Today, you can walk through history with a guided battlefield tour not only of what still stands, but what was.

ADDED STOPS IN TEXAS

1. Space Center Houston
2. Sixth Floor Museum at Dealey Plaza, Dallas
3. Cadillac Ranch, Amarillo
4. LBJ Presidential Library, Austin
5. Houston Livestock Show and Rodeo

The Alamo

FUN FACT:
Have you ever wondered where the Six Flags amusement parks got their names? Six flags—those of Spain, France, Mexico, the Republic of Texas, the Confederate States of America, and the United States—have flown over Texas.

"I must say as to what I have seen of Texas, it is the garden spot of the world. The best land, the best prospects for health I ever saw, and I do believe it is a fortune to any man to come here."

—DAVY CROCKETT

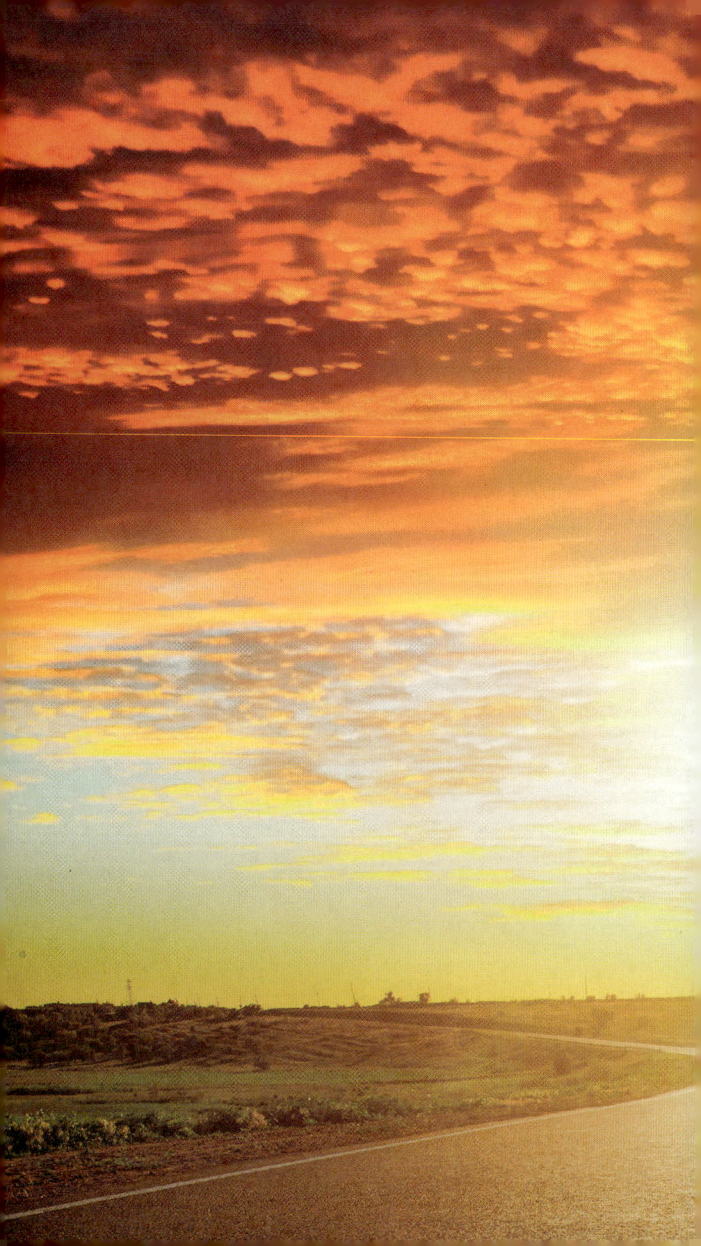

"Travel and change of place impart new vigor to the mind."

—SENECA

MIDWEST

Arkansas

Pit Stop:
Hot Springs National Park, Hot Springs

The smallest national park is also one of the most endearing, with bathing—not swimming, but actually taking a bath in an individual tub—encouraged. The National Park Service website conveniently breaks things down to one-hour, half-day, and all-day-or-more itineraries.

ADDED STOPS IN ARKANSAS

1. Crystal Bridges Museum of American Art, Bentonville
2. Little Rock Central High School, Little Rock
3. Clinton Presidential Center, Little Rock
4. Quigley's Castle, Eureka Springs
5. Mount Magazine State Park, Paris

Hot springs in the National Park

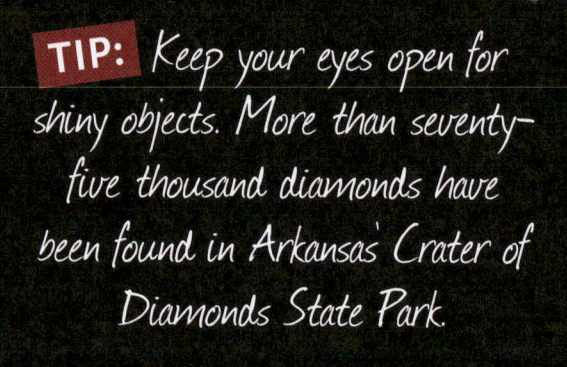

TIP: Keep your eyes open for shiny objects. More than seventy-five thousand diamonds have been found in Arkansas' Crater of Diamonds State Park.

FUN FACT:
The first woman elected to the U.S. Senate was Hattie Ophelia Caraway of Arkansas.

Missouri

Pit Stop:
Gateway Arch, St. Louis

The unmistakable landmark isn't just something cool to look at. It's also something cool to ride. Buy a timed ticket to take a tram ride to the top for a great view of the Mississippi River and beyond. And don't miss the Museum of Westward Expansion located underground below the arch.

The Gateway Arch

ADDED STOPS IN MISSOURI

1. Branson
2. Anheuser-Busch Brewery, St. Louis
3. Mark Twain Boyhood Home & Museum, Hannibal
4. Saint Louis Zoo
5. Pony Express Museum, St. Joseph

FUN FACT: Over one hundred species of animals roam the 281 acres of Grant's Farm, the former Busch Estate in St. Louis.

TIP: *Do you have a red suit in the closet that you wear only one day in December? Pack it if you plan on visiting Branson in July. The Discover Santa convention attracts thousands of St. Nick surrogates.*

Illinois

Pit Stop:
Millennium Park, Chicago

There are hundreds of free activities at Chicago's waterfront park, so some of the specifics of your visit will differ. But you can count on a great photo op at Anish Kapoor's "Cloud Gate" (aka the Jelly Bean), the unique Jaume Plensa "Crown Fountain" with its projected faces, the five-acre Lurie Garden, and the quirky Jay Pritzker Pavilion with its metallic ribbon-like stage frame.

The Cloud Gate sculpture at Millennium Park

Added Stops in Illinois

1.
Art Institute of Chicago

2.
Second City, Chicago

3.
Lincoln Home National Historic Site, Springfield

4.
Frank Lloyd Wright Home and Studio, Oak Park

5.
Anderson Japanese Gardens, Rockford

FUN FACT:
While Chicago has some of the tallest buildings in the United States, it also has one of the flattest landscapes. The highest natural point in the state is less than 1,250 feet above sea level.

"I ADORE CHICAGO. IT IS THE PULSE OF AMERICA."

—SARAH BERNHARDT

TIP: Visiting a college town? Be aware of move-in/move-out days. And also be aware of—and consider taking advantage of—the wealth of cultural activities available at most universities.

Indiana

Pit Stop:
Indianapolis Motor Speedway, Indianapolis

Call it the greatest spectacle in racing or the largest single-day sporting event in the world. Whatever you call it, the Indianapolis 500 is a stunning event and its home, the Indianapolis Motor Speedway, is remarkable even when a race isn't being run. The on-site Indianapolis Motor Speedway Museum tells the story and shows off the cars, while more adventurous visitors can take a ride around the track in a two-seater IndyCar Series racer.

The 98th annual Indianapolis 500

FUN FACT: The largest tabletop game convention in the world, Gen Con, attracts more than sixty-thousand players to Indianapolis annually.

ADDED STOPS IN INDIANA

1. Holiday World & Splashin' Safari, Santa Claus
2. The Children's Museum of Indianapolis
3. Conner Prairie Interactive History Park, Fishers
4. West Baden Springs Resort Hotel
5. Amish Acres Farm & Heritage Resort, Nappanee

In Indiana, Santa Claus is not just a jolly holiday figure. Santa Claus is also the name of the town where Holiday World & Splashin' Safari, home to world-class roller coasters, are located.

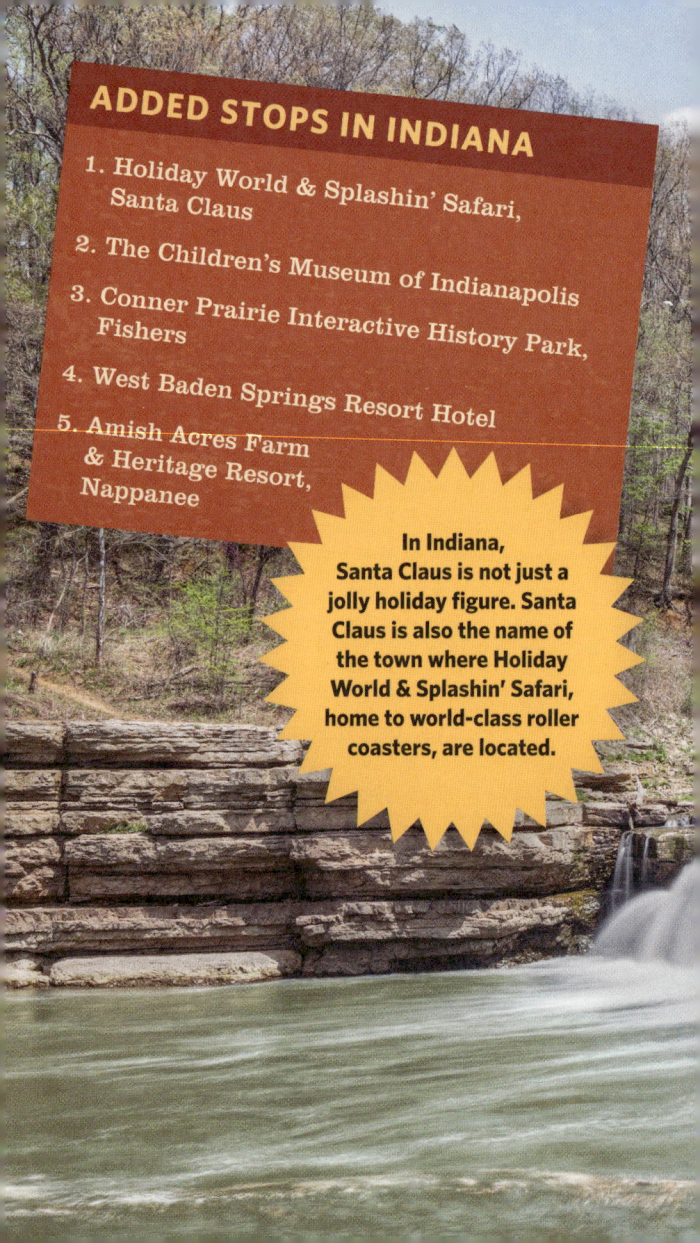

> "My father removed from Kentucky to Indiana, in my eighth year. It was a wild region..."
>
> —ABRAHAM LINCOLN

Ohio

Pit Stop:
Rock & Roll Hall of Fame, Cleveland

You may not be able to rock and roll all night and party every day, but you can visit the Rock & Roll Hall of Fame where the soundtrack of generations is honored. From ABBA to ZZ Top, more than three hundred musicians and behind-the-scenes movers and shakers have been inducted thus far. The permanent (and added to annually) hall of fame is supplemented with special exhibits and concerts, giving each visit its own unique vibe.

The Rock and Roll Hall of Fame

ADDED STOPS IN OHIO

1. Cedar Point Amusement Park, Sandusky
2. Football Hall of Fame, Canton
3. Cincinnati Zoo and Botanical Gardens
4. National Underground Railroad Freedom Center, Cincinnati
5. American Sign Museum, Cincinnati

FUN FACT:
Ohio is the only state with a non-rectangular flag.

TIP: Flying into Cincinnati? Don't be confused when you land in another state. The airport is just over the Kentucky border.

"Cincinnati is a beautiful city; cheerful, thriving, and animated. I have not often seen a place that commends itself so favourably and pleasantly to a stranger at the first glance as this does…"

—CHARLES DICKENS

Michigan

Pit Stop:
Henry Ford Museum/Greenfield Village, Dearborn

You don't have to be an automotive aficionado to appreciate this pair of Dearborn institutions. The Henry Ford Museum is less about cars than it is about innovation in all fields. A similar approach is taken at Greenfield Village, a living-history experience with eighty-three authentic historic structures and opportunities to get up close and personal with Abraham Lincoln, Noah Webster and, of course, Henry Ford.

ADDED STOPS IN MICHIGAN

1. Mackinac Island
2. Detroit Institute of the Arts, Detroit
3. Sleeping Bear Dunes National Lakeshore, Empire
4. Great Lakes Shipwreck Museum, Paradise
5. Frederick Meijer Gardens & Sculpture Park, Grand Rapids

Civil-war era re-enactors quilting at Greenfield Village

TIP: If you're in Detroit, you are **this close** to the Canadian border. If you want to take a quick trip to our neighbor to the north, make sure you have your passport with you and identification for any children in tow.

FUN FACT: The Gerald R. Ford Presidential Museum in Grand Rapids honors the only person who served as both President and Vice President without having been elected to either office.

Wisconsin

Pit Stop:
Wisconsin Dells

Time was when Wisconsin Dells was pretty much a summer experience for Midwesterners. But then one hotel decided to add an indoor waterpark. Then another decided to outdo it. And the ensuing waterpark war helped turn the Dells into a year-round getaway. There's plenty to do even if you didn't pack your swimming gear, with independent museums, attractions, amusement rides, and scenic tours.

Natural sandstone formations in Wisconsin Dells

ADDED STOPS IN WISCONSIN

1. Frank Lloyd Wright's Taliesin, Spring Green
2. Harley Davidson Museum, Milwaukee
3. National Freshwater Fishing Hall of Fame, Hayward
4. National Railroad Museum, Green Bay
5. The Packers' Lambeau Field, Green Bay

TIP: When packing, roll instead of fold. And remember that it's often better to spend a few hours at a local laundromat when on the road rather than drag along an extra suitcase.

FUN FACT:
Ninety percent of Wisconsin's milk is made into cheese. The state's cheesemakers produce more than six hundred varieties. Good news for Wisconsin: Per-capita cheese consumption in the United States is on the rise.

Minnesota

Pit Stop:
Guthrie Theater, Minneapolis

One of the pioneers of the regional professional theater movement, the Guthrie Theater helped spread the word that great theater wasn't limited to New York. Founded in 1963, it was designed from the beginning to bring the highest professional standards to classics and newer work. What started with just a summer season now employs more than five hundred people, producing work on three stages at its Riverfront District location overlooking the Mississippi River.

The Guthrie Theater

ADDED STOPS IN MINNESOTA

1. Lake Itacsa, headwaters of the Mississippi
2. Mall of America, Bloomington
3. Walker Art Center, Minneapolis
4. Cathedral of St. Paul, St. Paul
5. Hat-tossing Mary Tyler Moore Statue, Minneapolis

TIP: If you plan on passing a sizable city without stopping, try your best to avoid morning and evening rush hours. And don't forget to factor in time differences in your planning.

FUN FACT:
Looking for the North American mall with the most stores? Sorry, but you'll have to go across the border to the West Edmonton Mall in Canada. Mall of America still has the most shopping choices in the United States, though.

Iowa

Pit Stop:
Amana Colonies, Amana

The Amana Colonies, a National Historic Landmark, are the site of a group settlement of German Pietists who lived nearly self-sufficiently for eighty years. While the group's vision changed in the 1930s, the spirit of their independence survives in seven villages, attracting hundreds of thousands of visitors annually for a quaint, Old-World experience.

The unique architecture of Amana

ADDED STOPS IN IOWA

1. Field of Dreams, Dyersville
2. Grotto of the Redemption, West Bend
3. National Mississippi River Museum, Dubuque
4. American Gothic House Center, Eldon
5. Herbert Hoover Presidential Library and Museum, West Branch

Yes, the American Gothic House Center is the backdrop for the Grant Wood painting, one of the most famous paintings in America.

FUN FACT:
Rock and rollers know the story of Ozzy Osbourne and the bat. Well, it happened in Des Moines.

"I could never resist the call of the trail."

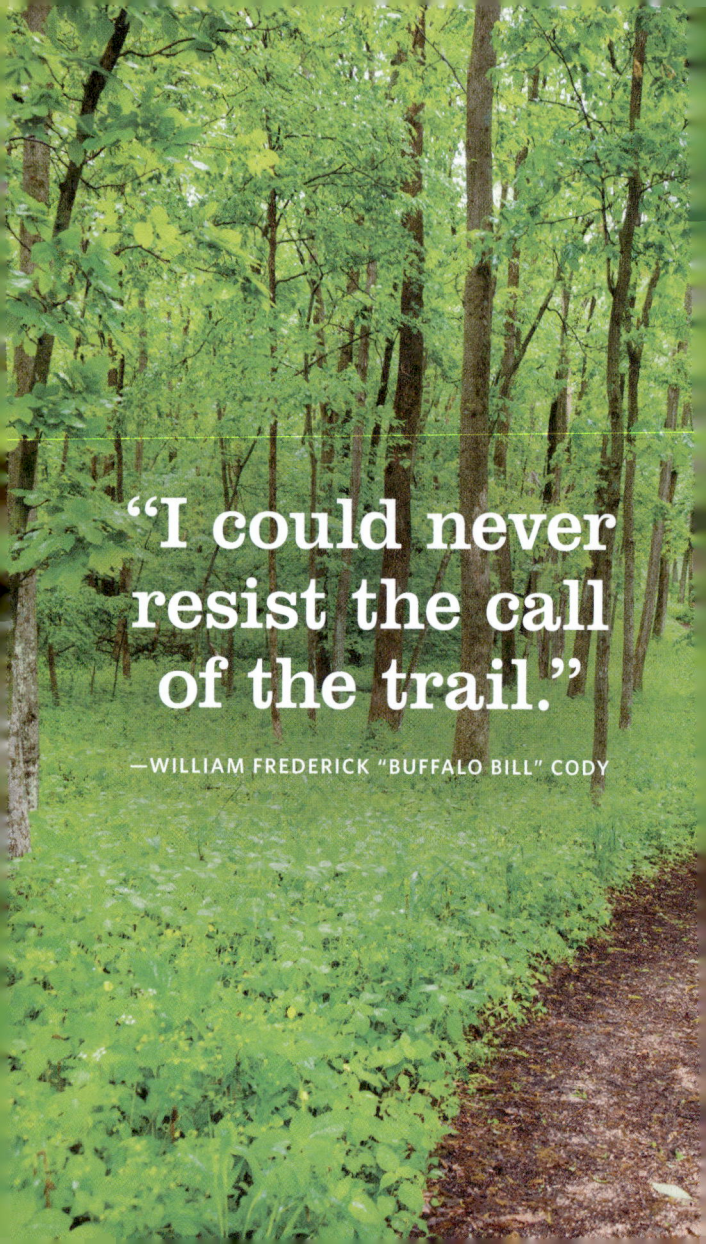

—WILLIAM FREDERICK "BUFFALO BILL" CODY

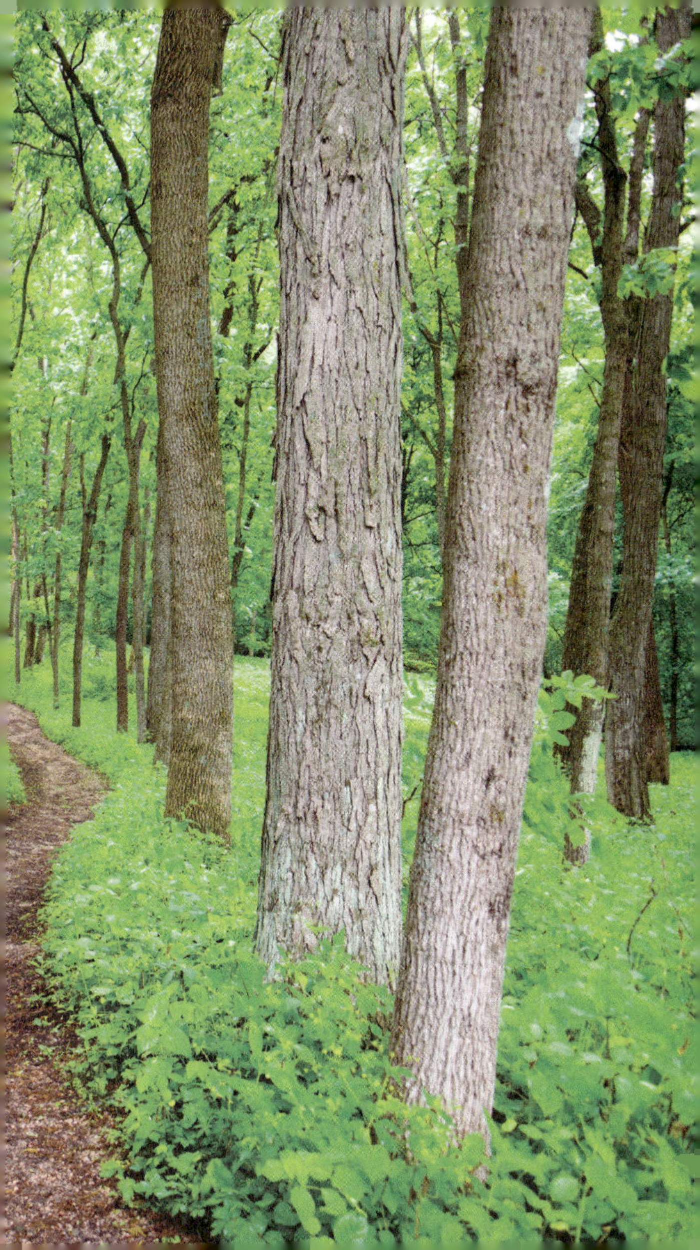

Oklahoma

Pit Stop:
National Cowboy & Western Heritage Museum, Oklahoma City

"The West begins here" claims this Oklahoma City institution. While it's possible to argue with the geography of that statement, you'd be hard-pressed to find a better place that tells the multifaceted story of the American West.

The back lawn of the Philbrook Museum

ADDED STOPS IN OKLAHOMA

1. Oklahoma City National Memorial
2. Cherokee Heritage Center, Park Hill
3. Museum of Osteology, Oklahoma City
4. Oklahoma City Zoo and Botanical Garden
5. Philbrook Museum of Art, Tulsa

The Museum of Osteology bills itself as the country's first museum of skeletons and boasts more than three hundred of them.

FUN FACT: The World Cow Chip Throwing Championship is held in Beaver, Oklahoma, every April.

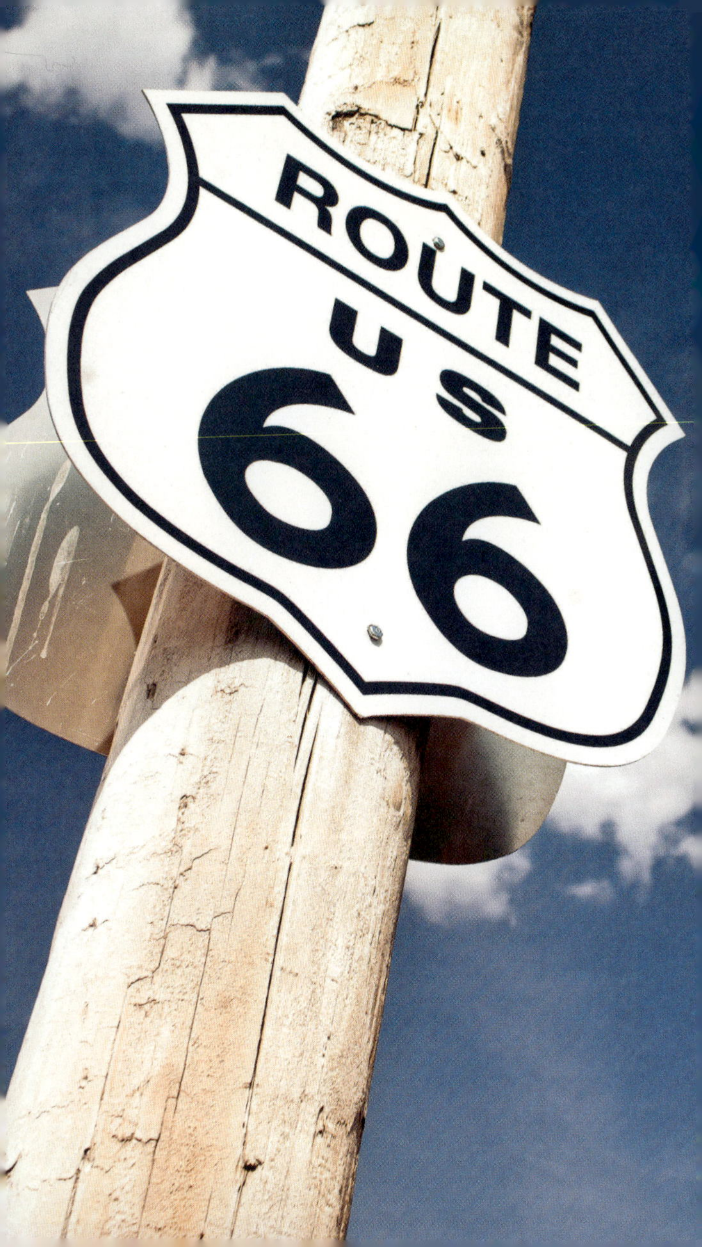
ROUTE
US
66

TIP: The longest driveable stretch of the famed Route 66 is through Oklahoma. But you don't have to stop at the first Route 66 museum you come across. Take your pick—the Oklahoma Route 66 Museum in Clinton, the National Transportation and Route 66 Museum in Elk City, the Route 66 Interpretive Center in Chandler, and the Route 66 Vintage Iron Motorcycle Museum in Miami.

Kansas

**Pit Stop:
The Geographic Center of the Contiguous United States (Sort Of), Lebanon**

Have you ever wanted to be in the center of everything? Well, you can come close by being at the geographic center of the connected forty-eight states. Pay a visit just outside Lebanon, Kansas. Don't expect a lot of activity: A stone marker and a small chapel mark the location, which, to be honest, isn't quite the exact location. That's in a former hog farm a half mile away.

Sign at the geographic center of the contiguous United States

ADDED STOPS IN KANSAS

1. Museum of World Treasures, Wichita
2. Brown v. Board of Education National Historic Site, Topeka
3. Kansas Underground Salt Museum, Hutchinson
4. Amelia Earhart Birthplace Museum, Atchison
5. Robert J. Dole Institute of Politics, Lawrence

The Scarecrow's pitchfork from *The Wizard of Oz* is in the Museum of World Treasures.

FUN FACT: Helium was discovered at the University of Kansas.

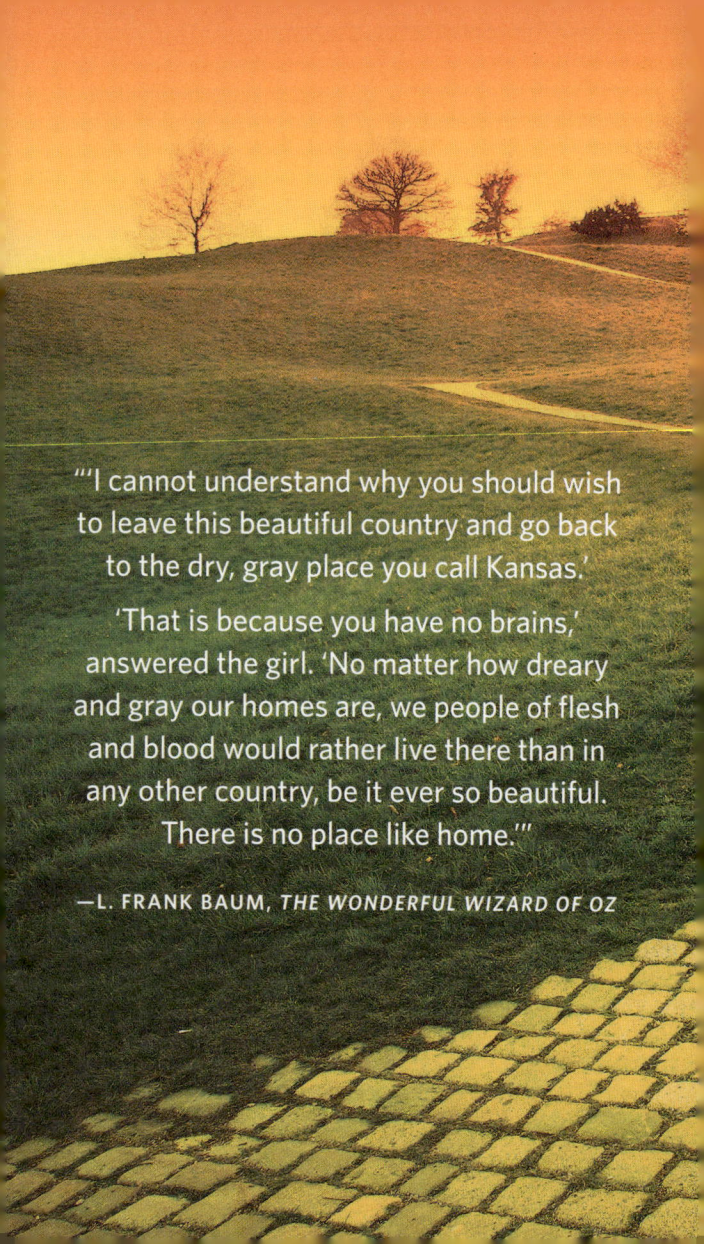

"'I cannot understand why you should wish to leave this beautiful country and go back to the dry, gray place you call Kansas.'

'That is because you have no brains,' answered the girl. 'No matter how dreary and gray our homes are, we people of flesh and blood would rather live there than in any other country, be it ever so beautiful. There is no place like home.'"

—L. FRANK BAUM, *THE WONDERFUL WIZARD OF OZ*

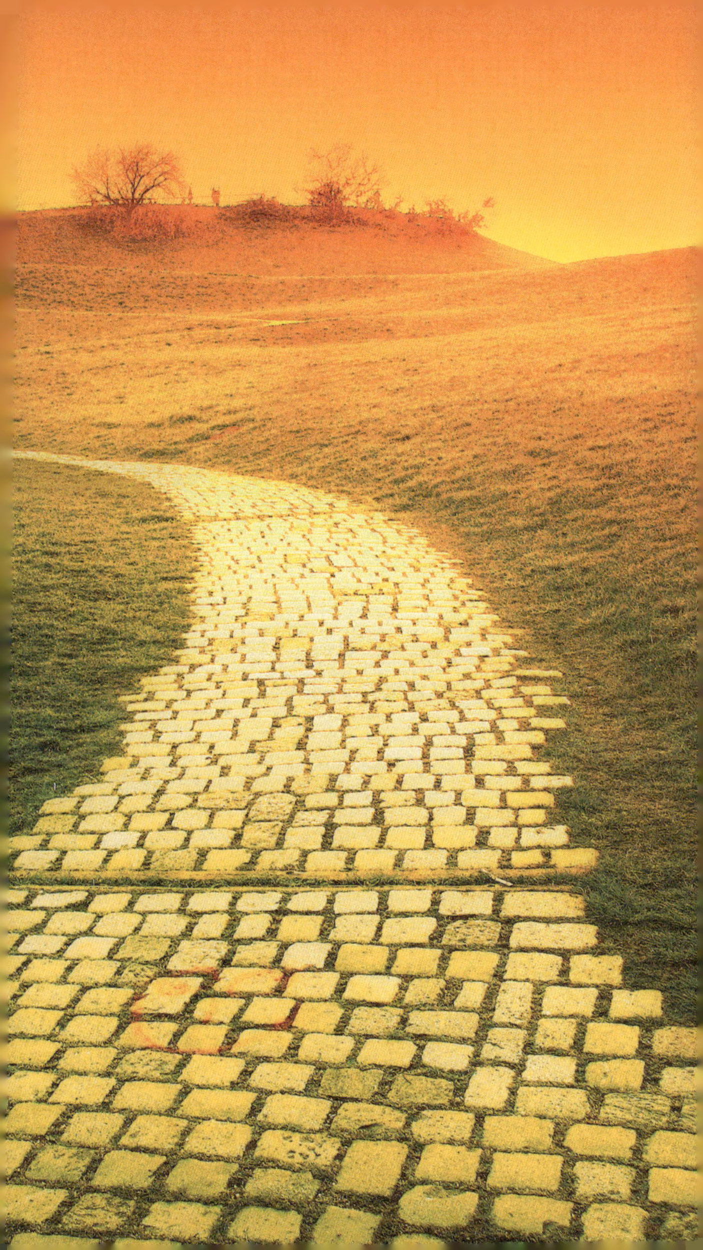

Nebraska

Pit Stop:
Chimney Rock National Historic Site, Bayard

The most famous landmark on the Oregon-California Trail, Chimney Rock has helped many a westbound pioneer find his or her way. Many of those travelers recorded their visits in drawings, writings, and photographs that can now be found in the collection on site. The landmark wasn't always known as Chimney Rock, though.

Chimney Rock National Historic Site

ADDED STOPS IN NEBRASKA

1. Ashfall Fossil Beds, Royal
2. Joslyn Castle, Omaha
3. Homestead National Monument of America, Beatrice
4. Scotts Bluff National Monument, Gering
5. Stuhr Museum of the Prairie Pioneer, Grand Island

FUN FACT:
Fun Fact: Kool-Aid was invented in Hastings, Nebraska.

TIP: Back up your smartphone photos or send them directly to the cloud. You don't want your memories to disappear in the case of a lost phone.

> "A journey of a thousand miles begins with a single step."
>
> —LAO TZU

North Dakota

Pit Stop:
International Peace Garden, U.S.-Canadian Border

Technically, this is only partly a U.S. attraction. That's because its 3.65 square miles are parked on the international border between North Dakota and Manitoba, Canada. Flying the flags of the Maple Leaf and the Stars and Stripes since the park was dedicated in 1932, the gardens have expanded over the years with a floral clock (covered in up to five thousand plants, with its design changed annually), water gardens, and a dramatic bell tower. A pair of floral flags are the only designs that remain consistent from year to year.

ADDED STOPS IN NORTH DAKOTA

1. Theodore Roosevelt National Park
2. Fort Abraham Lincoln, Mandan
3. Dakota Dinosaur Museum, Dickinson
4. Bonanzaville, West Fargo
5. North Dakota Lewis and Clark Interpretive Center, Washburn

FUN FACT:
Ninety percent of North Dakota is composed of farms, making it the most rural of the fifty states.

Towers at the International Peace Garden

South Dakota

Pit Stop:
Badlands National Park

Not only are you encouraged to look up at the night sky when visiting Badlands National Park, you can also borrow a telescope to get an even closer look. There's plenty to see by day as well, including hikes through the park's prairie landscape or more rugged uphill adventures. Keep an eye out for American bison and Rocky Mountain bighorn sheep.

ADDED STOPS IN SOUTH DAKOTA

1. Mount Rushmore National Memorial, Keystone
2. Crazy Horse Memorial (in progress), Crazy Horse
3. Mitchell Corn Palace, Mitchell
4. The Journey Museum & Learning Center, Rapid City
5. Reptile Gardens, Rapid City

Badlands National Park

FUN FACT:
Want to see a five-hundred-year-old cello? The National Music Museum in Vermillion has one of the largest and most important collections of musical instruments in the world.

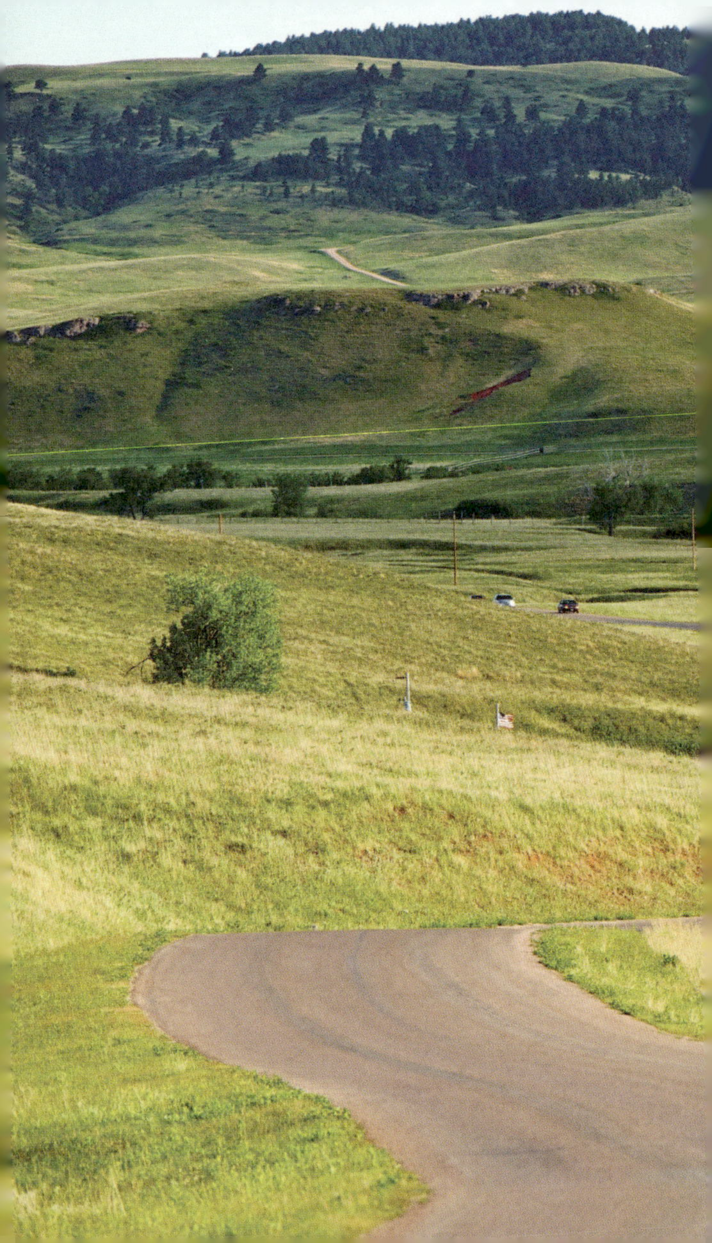

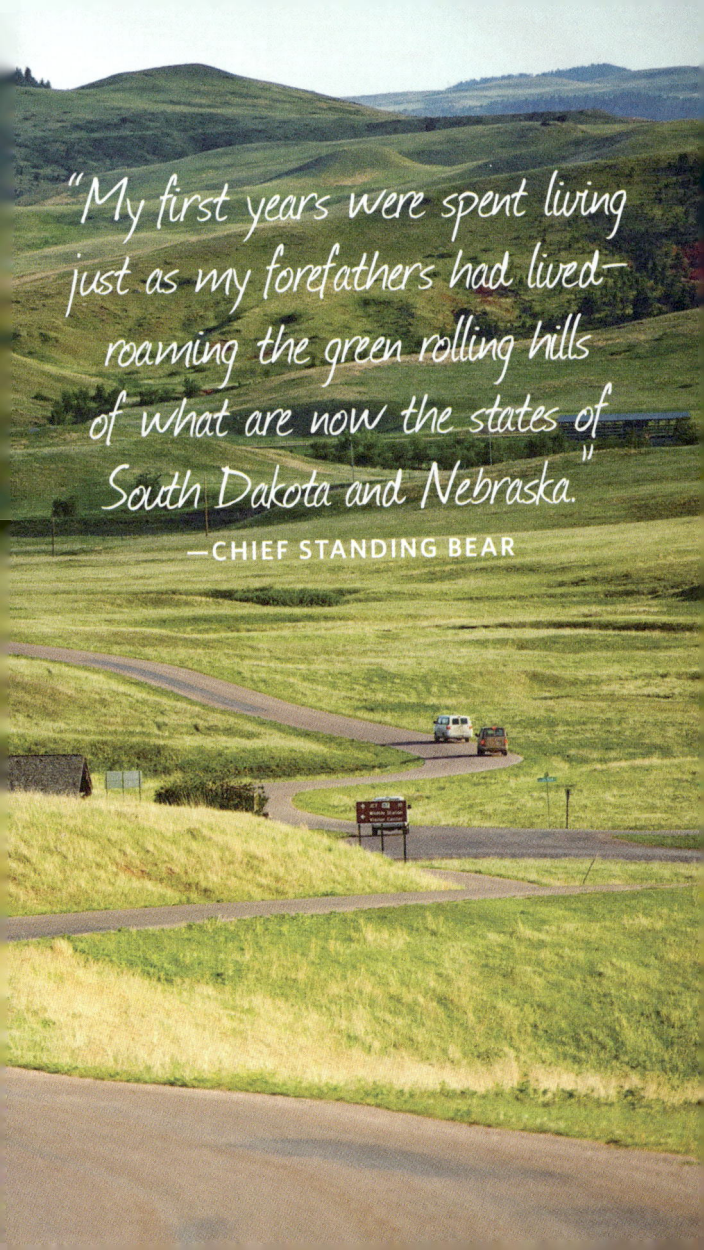

"My first years were spent living just as my forefathers had lived—roaming the green rolling hills of what are now the states of South Dakota and Nebraska."

—CHIEF STANDING BEAR

MOUNTAIN STATES

Montana

**Pit Stop:
Glacier National Park**

Take your pick of more than seven hundred miles of hiking trails through the Rocky Mountains, join a ranger-led program ranging from a leisurely walk to a boat tour, enjoy license-free trout fishing, or catch one of the summer Native America Speaks programs to learn from Blackfeet, Salish, Kootenai, and Pend d'Oreille tribal members.

St. Mary Lake in Glacier National Park

ADDED STOPS IN MONTANA

1. Little Bighorn Battlefield National Monument, Crow Agency
2. Museum of the Rockies, Bozeman
3. World Museum of Mining, Butte
4. American Computer & Robotics Museum, Bozeman
5. National Bison Range, Moiese

FUN FACT:
The tradition of placing Gideon Bibles in motel rooms began in Montana.

TIP:

Whether you are camping or "glamping" (bringing some of the comforts of home with you on your trip), keep these recommendations in mind:

- Get organized first—especially if there's a chance you are going to arrive at your campsite after dark.

- If you want more solitude, be ready to hike beyond the car campers.

- Get the fire going as soon as you set up camp.

- Bring enough food to share. You never know what friends you'll make. And don't forget the pleasure of a good breakfast.

- Your pillow matters more than your sleeping bag when it comes to getting a good night's semi-sleep.

- If you snore, keep a respectful distance from other tents.
- Make sure to have trash bags on hand. Leave nothing behind.
- If you know how to play guitar, by all means bring it. Just don't put on a show unless asked.
- Block ice stays colder longer than cubed. It could mean the difference between a next-day cold drink and a lukewarm one.
- Keep your camp organized. You don't want to spend hiking time searching for a missing item. And you don't want to have to spend hours back home sorting everything out afterwards.

Wyoming

Pit Stop:
Yellowstone National Park

The world's first national park remains one of its most striking—and most popular. Brace yourself for crowds, at least at the entry points and popular spots, during summer months. But don't let that deter you. This is a stunning, varied park containing the largest concentration of wildlife in the Lower 48, and about half the active geysers in the world. (Don't miss Old Faithful.)

ADDED STOPS IN WYOMING

1. Devil's Tower, near Sundance
2. Grand Teton National Park
3. Buffalo Bill Center of the West, Cody
4. Museum of the Mountain Man, Pinedale
5. National Museum of Wildlife Art, Jackson

FUN FACT:
When James Cash Penney died at age ninety-five in 1971, he left behind eighteen hundred J.C. Penney stores. The first one, referred to as "the mother store," can be found in Kammerer.

Yellowstone National Park

> "There can be nothing in the world more beautiful than the Yosemite, the groves of the giant sequoias and redwoods, the Canyon of the Colorado, the Canyon of the Yellowstone, the Three Tetons; and our people should see to it that they are preserved for their children and their children's children forever, with their majestic beauty all unmarred."
>
> —THEODORE ROOSEVELT

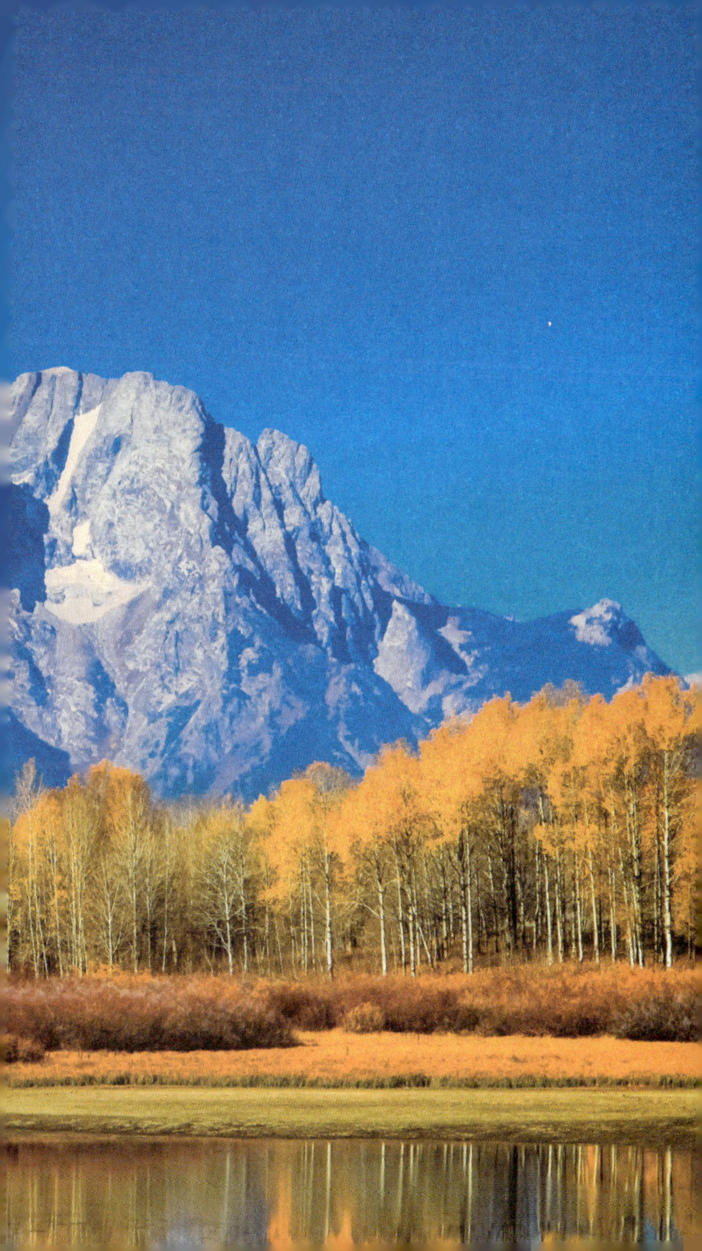

Idaho

Pit Stop:
Sun Valley

Okay, your first thought may be skiing. And that's certainly key to the popularity of Sun Valley. But you can also catch a movie in a 1930s opera house, take a spa treatment, and stay in a historic lodge in and around your time spent fly fishing, golfing, hiking, biking, sleigh riding, and even catching an ice show at this Idaho hotspot.

Sun Valley

ADDED STOPS IN IDAHO

1. Crater of the Moon National Monument and Preserve, Arco
2. Old Idaho State Penitentiary, Boise
3. Idaho Potato Museum, Blackfoot
4. World Center for Birds of Prey, Boise
5. Snake River Stampede Rodeo, Nampa

FUN FACT:
Don't sweat it—even longtime residents of Idaho don't agree on where the name comes from.

Nevada

**Pit Stop:
The Las Vegas Strip**

Whether you've got a gambling streak or just a hunger for buffet meals, a trip to Vegas is a compulsory experience—provided you can control your compulsions. Awash with neon, the can-you-top-this approach has turned the Strip into a visual candy store. And thanks to an effective ad campaign, your friends back home will understand if you don't tell them everything that happened to you there.

The Las Vegas Strip

TWO QUICK VEGAS TIPS:

1. Only take into a casino what you can afford to lose.

2. Repeat number 1.

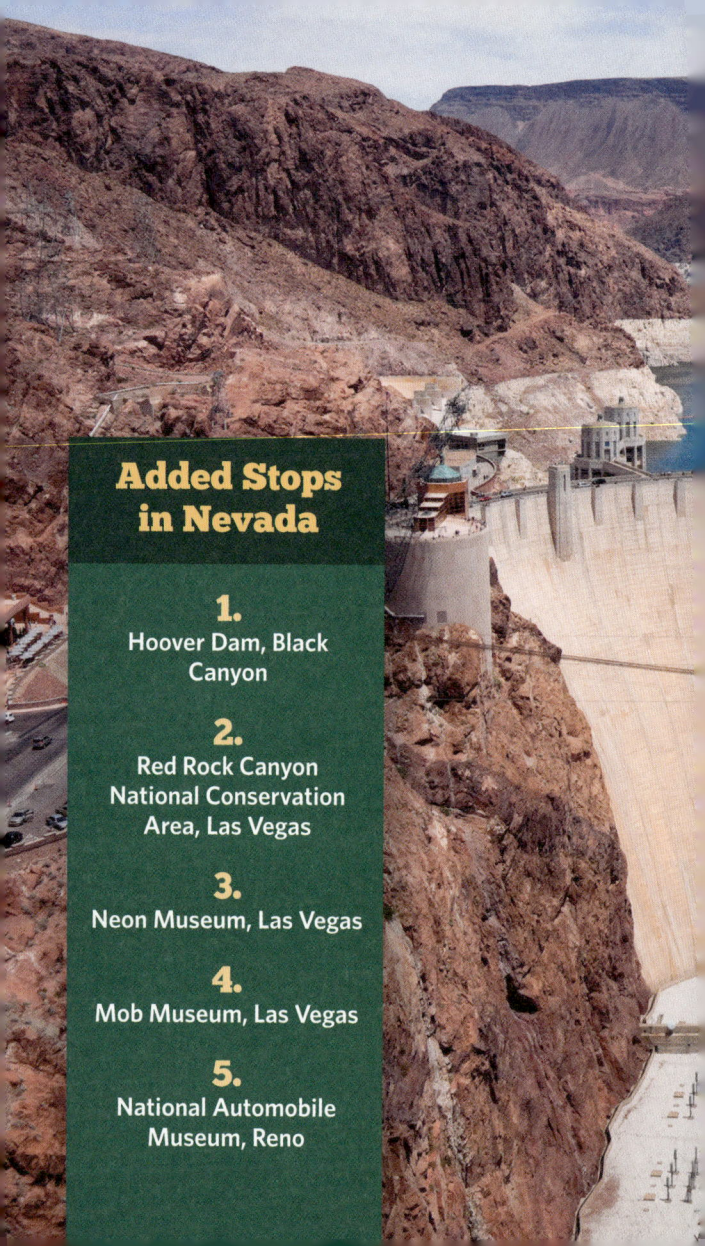

Added Stops in Nevada

1.
Hoover Dam, Black Canyon

2.
Red Rock Canyon National Conservation Area, Las Vegas

3.
Neon Museum, Las Vegas

4.
Mob Museum, Las Vegas

5.
National Automobile Museum, Reno

FUN FACT: There's enough concrete in the Hoover Dam to pave a road from New York City to San Francisco.

"LIKE ALL GREAT TRAVELERS, I HAVE SEEN MORE THAN I REMEMBER, AND REMEMBER MORE THAN I HAVE SEEN."

—BENJAMIN DISRAELI

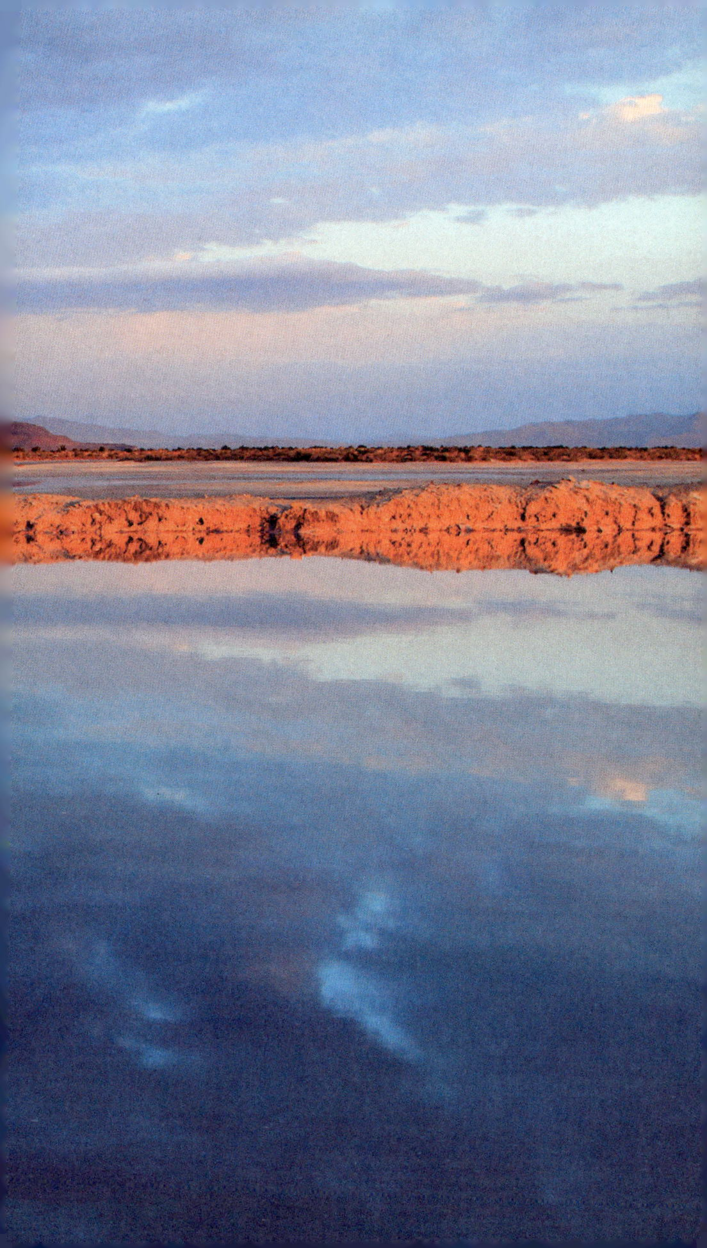

SOUTHWEST

Utah

Pit Stop:
Temple Square, Salt Lake City

No matter what your faith, the centerpiece of Salt Lake City is an architectural, floral, historical site to behold. Catch a performance by the Mormon Tabernacle Choir on its home turf, tour Salt Lake Temple, or do some genealogy work at the FamilySearch Center. A pair of visitors' centers are open to guide you.

Salt Lake Temple in Temple Square

ADDED STOPS IN UTAH

1. Zion National Park
2. Bryce Canyon National Park
3. Monument Valley Navajo Tribal Park, Oljato-Monument Valley
4. Golden Spike National Historic Site, Brigham City
5. Great Salt Lake

The Great Salt Lake is, true to its name, very salty—four times that of any of the oceans.

"TRAVEL BRINGS POWER AND LOVE BACK INTO YOUR LIFE."
—RUMI

Colorado

Pit Stop:
Pikes Peak, Cascade

It may sound intimidating—as if only the most avid mountaineers should visit. But while it's more than 14,000 feet above sea level, Pikes Peak can also be experienced via the Broadmoor Pikes Peak Cog Railway. Or you can just drive the nineteen-mile scenic route through the clouds to the top.

Sign at Pikes Peak

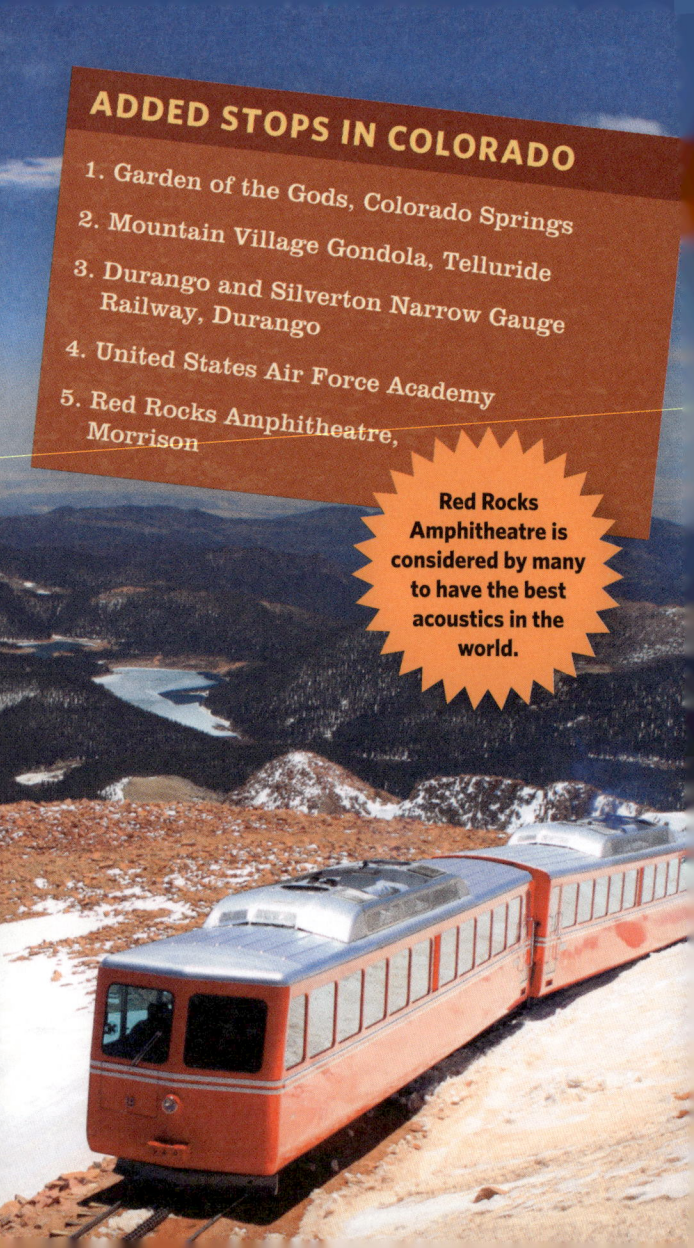

ADDED STOPS IN COLORADO

1. Garden of the Gods, Colorado Springs
2. Mountain Village Gondola, Telluride
3. Durango and Silverton Narrow Gauge Railway, Durango
4. United States Air Force Academy
5. Red Rocks Amphitheatre, Morrison

Red Rocks Amphitheatre is considered by many to have the best acoustics in the world.

TIP: Altitude can affect attitude—and a lot more. Drinking lots of water helps mitigate the effects, as does eating high-potassium foods. You are also more likely to get sunburned, which means stepping up sun protection.

FUN FACT: About 75 percent of U.S. land area over 10,000 feet in altitude is in Colorado.

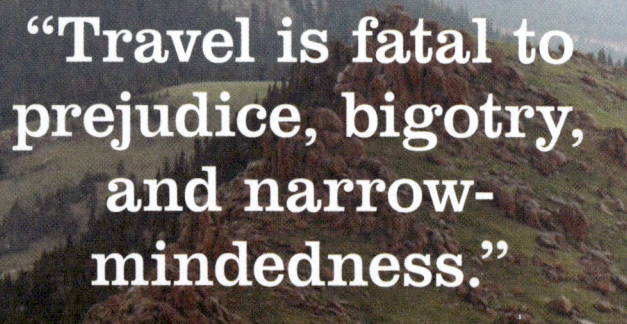

> "Travel is fatal to prejudice, bigotry, and narrow-mindedness."
>
> —MARK TWAIN

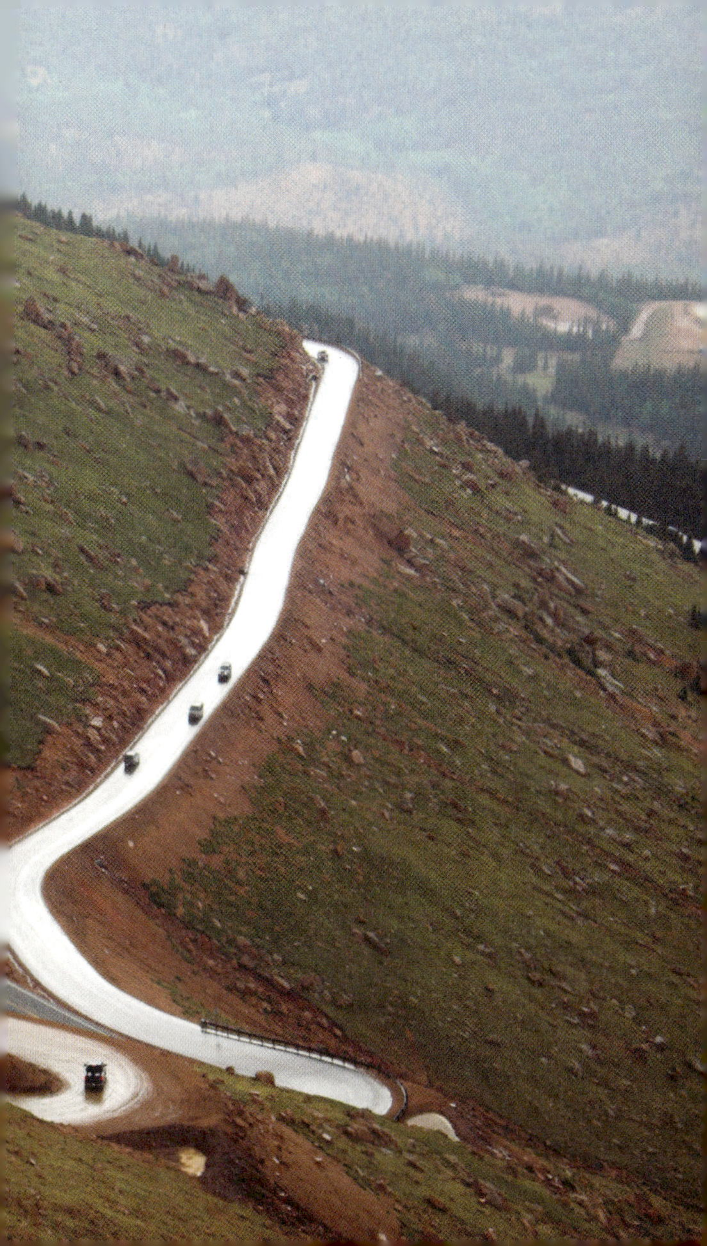

New Mexico

**Pit Stop:
Carlsbad Caverns National Park,
Carlsbad**

The one hundred nineteen known caves in Carlsbad Caverns are amazing in and of themselves, but for a truly unforgettable experience, stop by at dusk or dawn to see about a quarter of a million bats in grand spirals entering and exiting.

FUN FACT:
Just because many of the buildings in New Mexico are made from adobe doesn't mean that architecture here is old news. Early Pueblo architecture exists near Spanish Colonial, Greek Revival elements can be found in territorial buildings, and, in the twentieth century, new underlying building materials made larger structures possible.

Crystal Spring Dome at Carlsbad Caverns National Park

ADDED STOPS IN NEW MEXICO

1. Chaco Culture National Historical Park, Nageezi
2. Georgia O'Keeffe Museum, Santa Fe
3. White Sands National Monument, Chihuahuan Desert
4. Very Large Array Radio Astronomy Observatory, Socorro
5. Bandelier National Monument, Los Alamos

Albuquerque Balloon Festival

TIP: Time your trip for the Albuquerque Balloon Festival. Yes, it features the expected light-bulb-shaped hot air balloons, but past fests have included such wonders as balloons in the shape of a birthday cake, a treehouse, and a brain.

Arizona

**Pit Stop:
The Grand Canyon,
Grand Canyon Village**

In a state packed with visual splendor, the Grand Canyon—carved over time by the Colorado River—still stands out as a bucket-list spot for both U.S. residents and international travelers. Traditionally, the south rim has been the most popular visitation point, but thanks to the new Grand Canyon Skywalk—a curved, glass-floored bridge extending dizzyingly over midair—the west rim has become a hotspot for daytrippers.

Toroweap Overlook in the Grand Canyon National Park

"The wonders of the Grand Canyon cannot be adequately represented in symbols of speech, nor by speech itself."

—JOHN WESLEY POWELL

Added Stops in Arizona

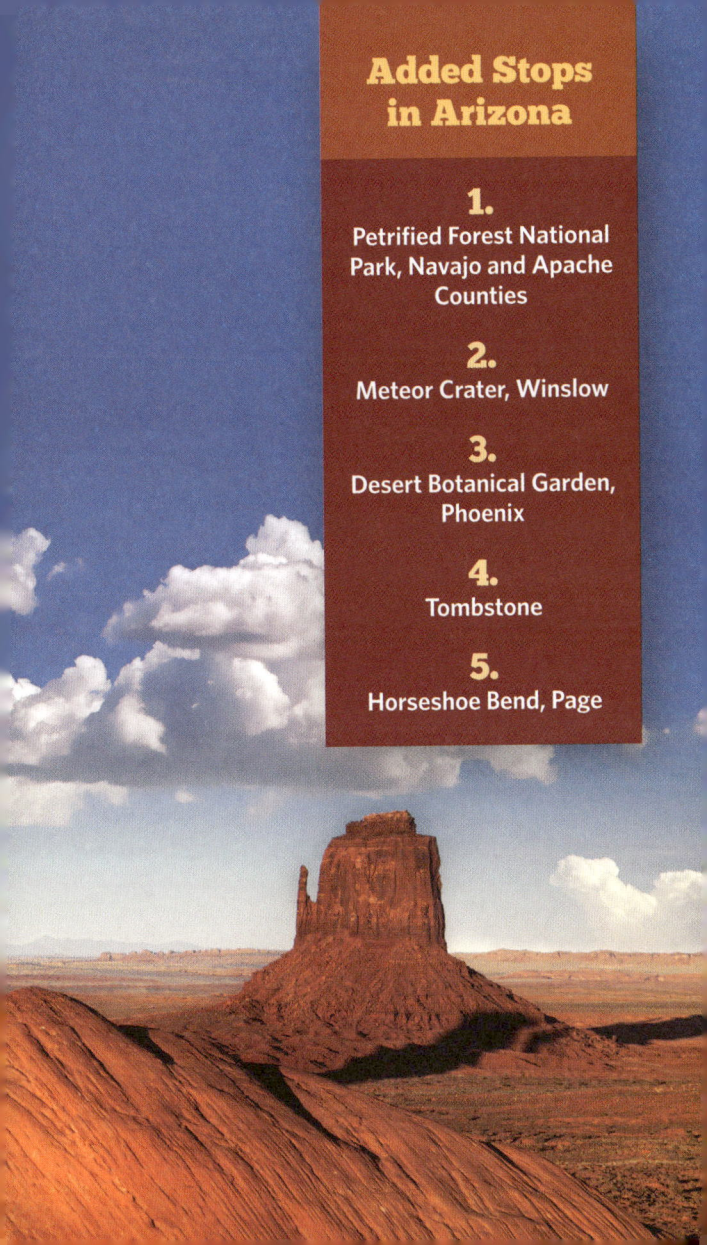

1.
Petrified Forest National Park, Navajo and Apache Counties

2.
Meteor Crater, Winslow

3.
Desert Botanical Garden, Phoenix

4.
Tombstone

5.
Horseshoe Bend, Page

"Adventure is worthwhile."

—AESOP

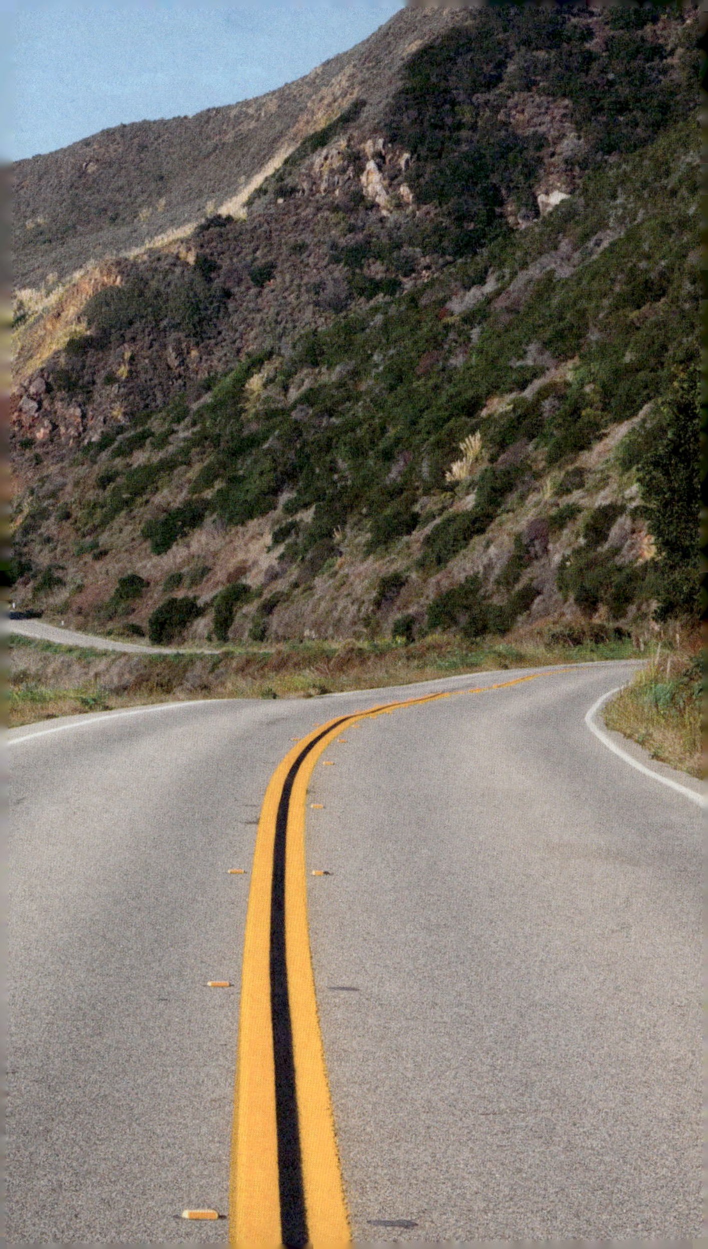

WEST COAST

California

Pit Stop:
Hollywood

Why are so many people looking down while they walk through Hollywood? No doubt they are reading the names on the Hollywood Walk of Fame or measuring their footprints against those of the cement imprints in front of the iconic TCL Chinese Theatre. But that's just the beginning. Here, and in studios in surrounding communities, you can be an audience member for your favorite sitcom or game show (free, but advance tickets needed). If the timing is right, you might even get a glimpse of your favorite star at a red-carpet event.

FUN FACT: When scared, California condors throw up.

The landmark Hollywood Sign

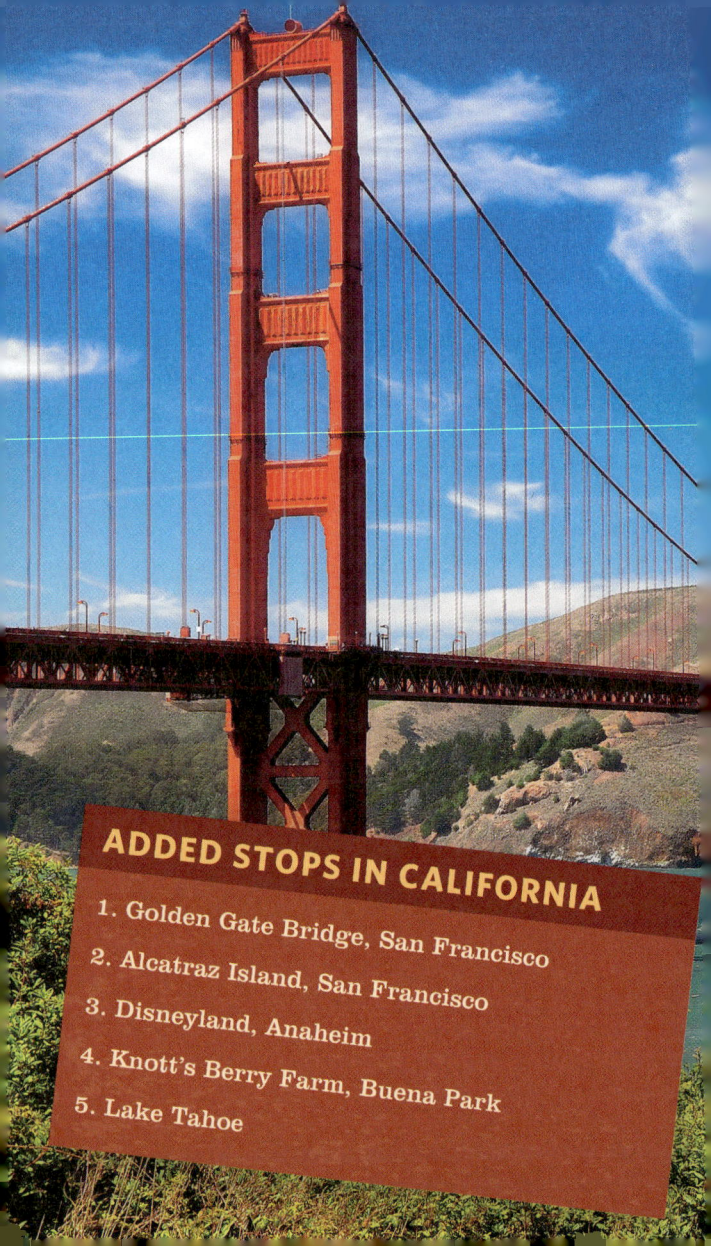

ADDED STOPS IN CALIFORNIA

1. Golden Gate Bridge, San Francisco
2. Alcatraz Island, San Francisco
3. Disneyland, Anaheim
4. Knott's Berry Farm, Buena Park
5. Lake Tahoe

TIP: It may be tempting when stuck in California traffic, but remember that it is against the law to write, send or read text-based messages while driving. Further, drivers must use a hands-free device when using a mobile phone.

"THE MAN WHO GOES ALONE CAN START TODAY; BUT HE WHO TRAVELS WITH ANOTHER MUST WAIT 'TIL THAT OTHER IS READY."

-HENRY DAVID THOREAU

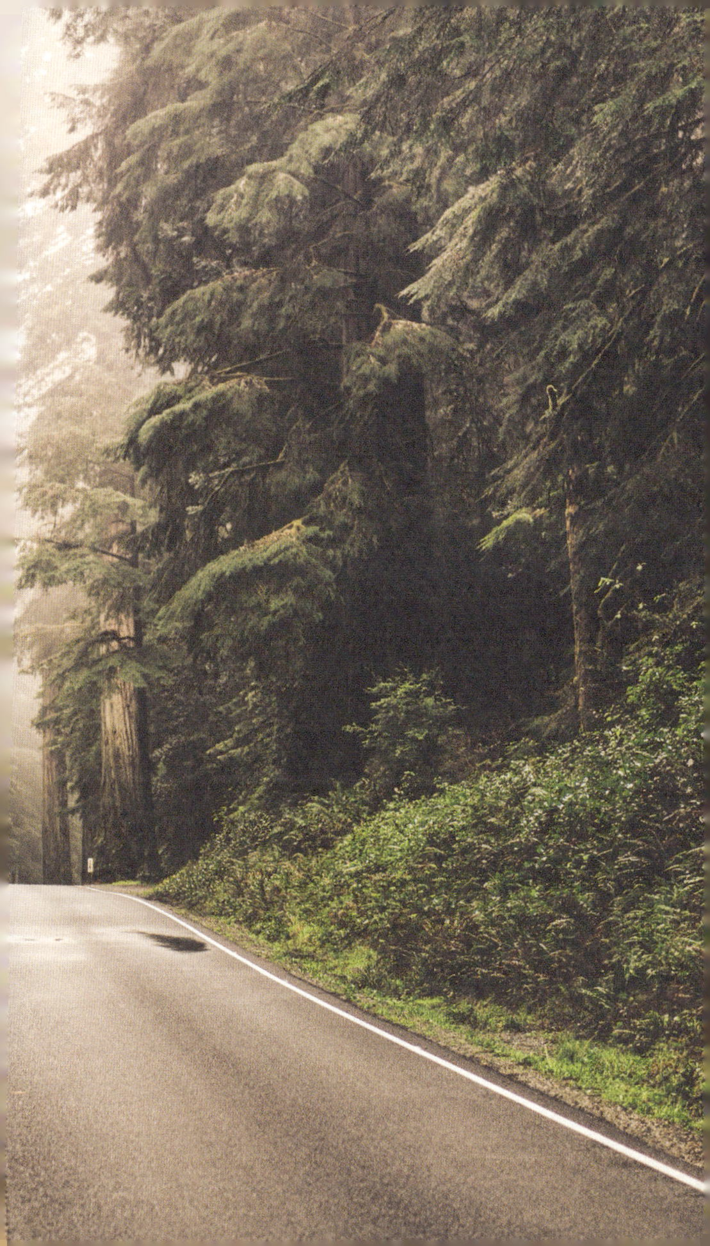

Oregon

Pit Stop:
Oregon Shakespeare Festival, Ashland

Running from February through November each year, the Oregon Shakespeare Festival offers world-class productions from the Bard and beyond. Two indoor stages and one outdoor house the plays themselves, but visitors can also take in backstage tours, park talks, lectures, classes, workshops, and pre- and post-show conversations with the on- and offstage talent. If visiting in the summer, make sure to take in a free outdoor Green Show featuring different talent each night before the evening performances.

Crater Lake National Park

ADDED STOPS IN OREGON

1. Crater Lake National Park
2. Multnomah Falls
3. Oregon Zoo, Portland
4. High Desert Museum, Bend
5. World Forestry Center, Portland

FUN FACT:
Brush up on your do-si-do—the official state dance of Oregon is the square dance.

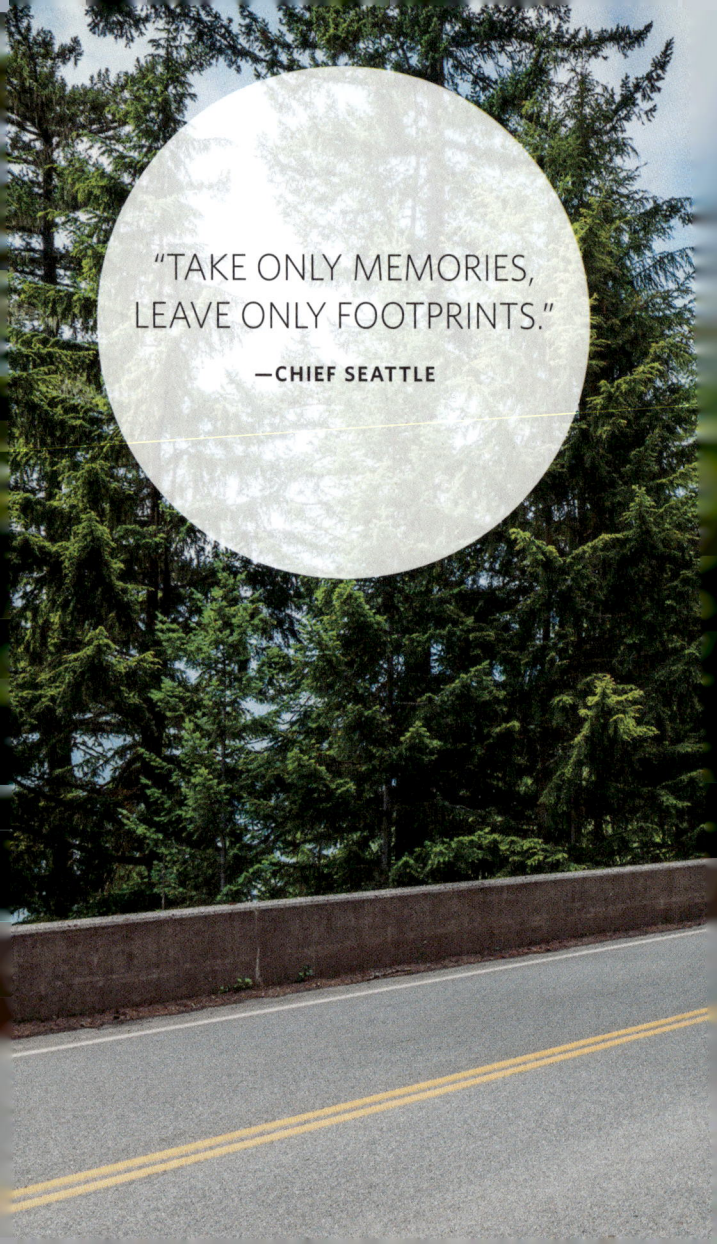

> "TAKE ONLY MEMORIES,
> LEAVE ONLY FOOTPRINTS."
>
> —CHIEF SEATTLE

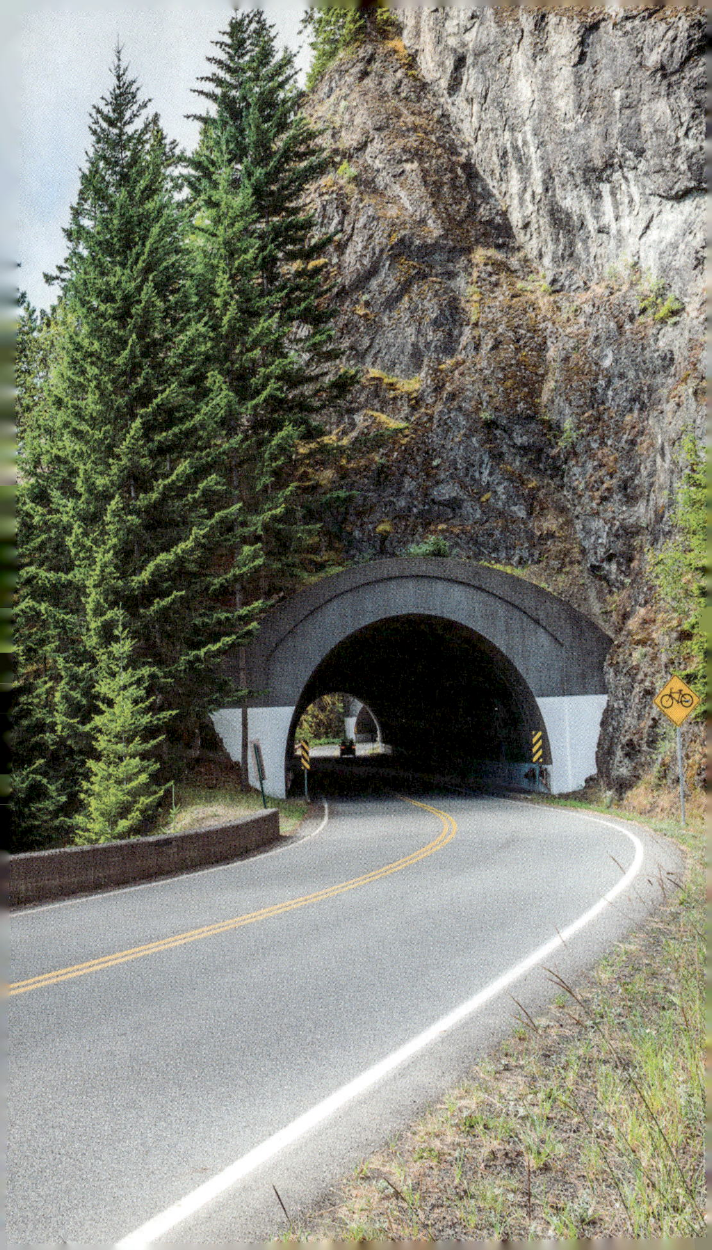

Washington

Pit Stop:
Pike Place Market, Seattle

Great cities have great public markets. And there's none greater than this Seattle treasure. One of the country's oldest farmers' markets, it covers nine acres, with every step a new sensory feast. The fish markets are a must, of course, but you'll also want to take a photo with Rachel the 550-pound piggy bank, join the audience of busking performers, or try a cooking demonstration in the Atrium Kitchen.

ADDED STOPS IN WASHINGTON

1. Space Needle, Seattle
2. Mount St. Helens
3. Museum of Glass, Tacoma
4. Leavenworth Bavarian Village
5. Grand Coulee Dam

FUN FACT: Up to twelve thousand horses run free on Washington's Yakima Indian Reservation.

Rachel the 550-pound bronze pig

TIP: Don't put your home address on your luggage tags. Better to use a workplace address and a covered tag.

"It is not down in any map; true places never are."

—HERMAN MELVILLE

Alaska

Pit Stop:
Denali National Park and Preserve

The area formerly known as Mt. McKinley and still the undisputed highest spot in North America (at 20,310 feet), Denali has one ninety-two-mile stretch of road going through six million acres. Yes, million. Don't look for fences here, but keep an eye out for moose, caribou, Dall sheep, wolves, and grizzly bears.

ADDED STOPS IN ALASKA

1. Juneau Icefield, Juneau
2. Tracy Arm Fjord, near Juneau
3. Klondike Gold Rush National Historical Park, Skagway
4. Alaska Native Heritage Center, Anchorage
5. Hammer Museum, Haines

FUN FACT:
Alaska cost the United States $7.2 million—not bad when you consider that's two cents per acre.

Moose Bull at Denali National Park

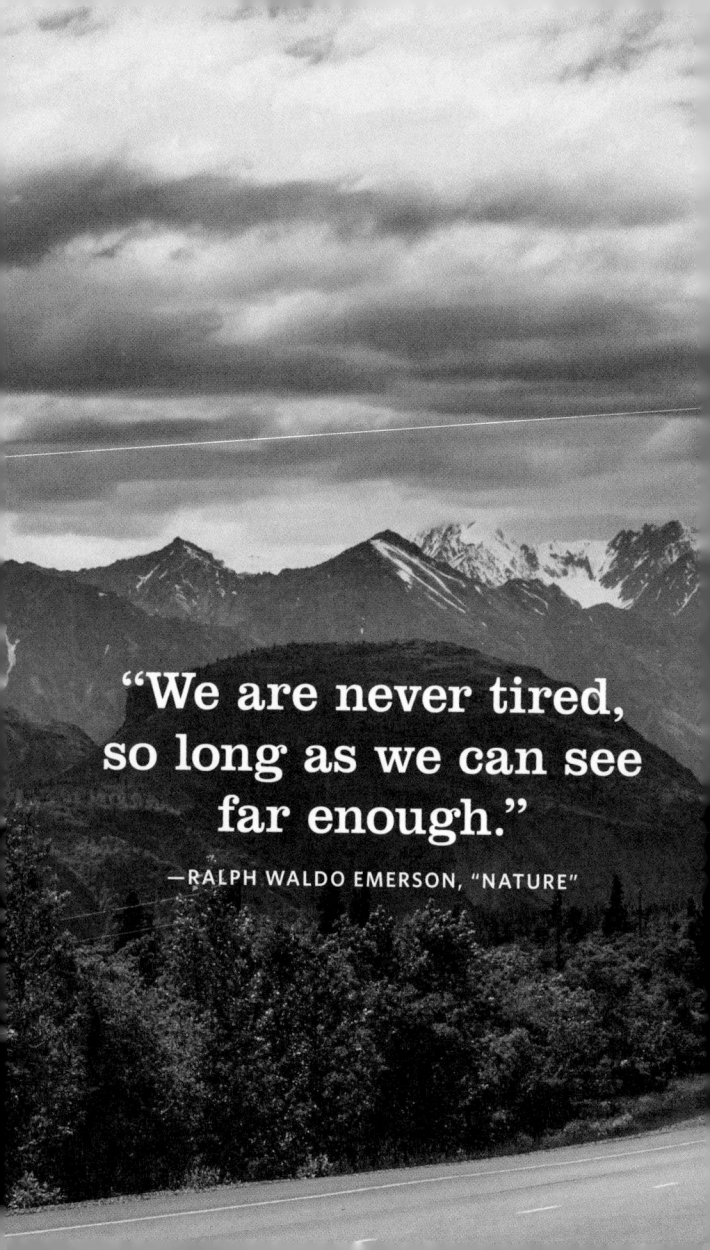

"We are never tired, so long as we can see far enough."

—RALPH WALDO EMERSON, "NATURE"

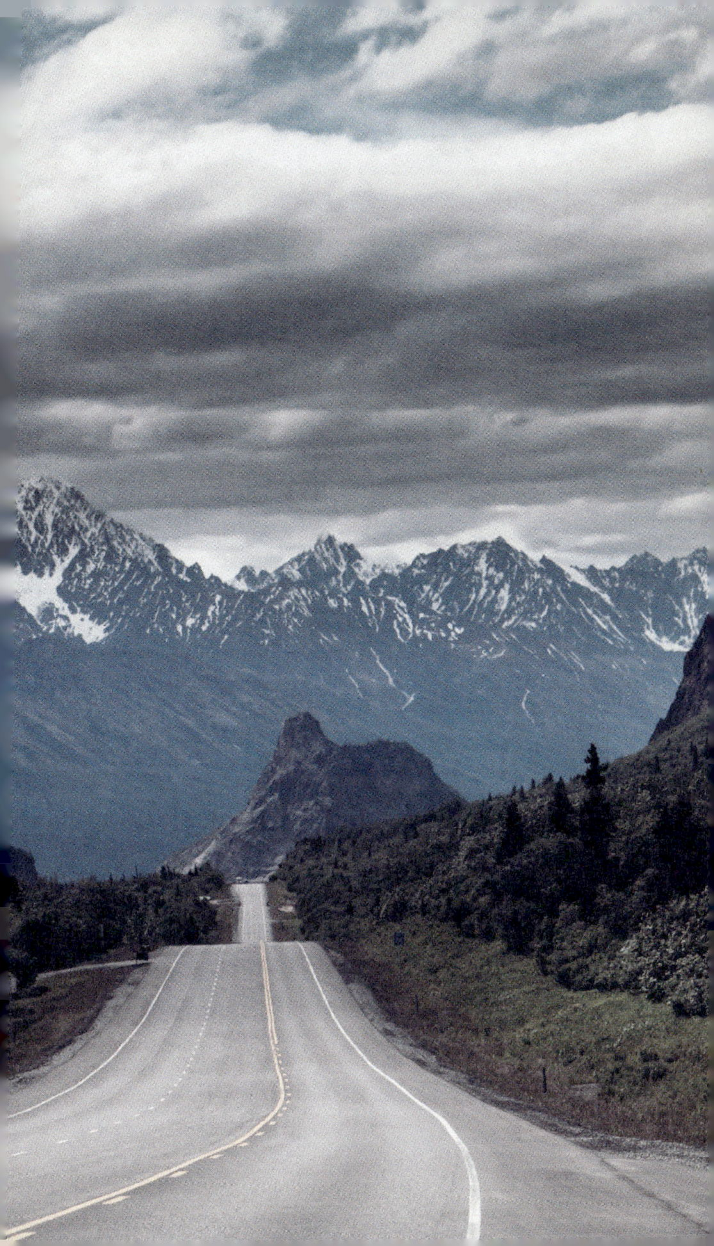

Hawaii

Pit Stop:
Punaluu Black Sand Beach, Hawaii Island, Kau Coast

You probably have never seen anything like this natural phenomenon, caused by the constant volcanic activity in the area. There's a good chance you'll see a Hawaiian green sea turtle as well. (Hands off, though—the turtles, like the sand, can't be taken home.) The beach is near Hawaii Volcanoes National Park, home of the Kilauea volcano.

ADDED STOPS IN HAWAII

1. Pearl Harbor and USS *Arizona* Memorial, Oahu
2. Diamond Head, Honolulu
3. Polynesian Cultural Center, Laie
4. Waimoku Falls, Maui
5. Dole Plantation, Wahiawa

TIP: *Quantities are limited for rental cars in Hawaii. Book early.*

FUN FACT: Hawaii is the only state with a tropical rainforest.

Turtles at Punaluu Black Sand Beach

"The world is a book, and those who do not travel read only one page."

—SAINT AUGUSTINE

IF YOU HAVE ENJOYED THIS BOOK
OR IT HAS TOUCHED YOUR LIFE IN SOME WAY,
WE WOULD LOVE TO HEAR FROM YOU.

Please send your comments to:
Hallmark Book Feedback
P.O. Box 419034
Mail Drop 100
Kansas City, MO 64141

Or e-mail us at:
booknotes@hallmark.com